Lisa Freigang

Formations of Identity in Salman Rushdie's Fictions

Lisa Freigang

Formations of Identity in Salman Rushdie's Fictions

Tectum Verlag

Lisa Freigang

Formations of Identity in Salman Rushdie's Fictions
ISBN: 978-3-8288-2065-4
Umschlagabbildung - cybernautin : www.photocase.com

Besuchen Sie uns im Internet
www.tectum-verlag.de

Bibliografische Informationen der Deutschen Nationalbibliothek
Die Deutsche Nationalbibliothek verzeichnet diese Publikation in der Deutschen Nationalbibliografie; detaillierte bibliografische Angaben sind im Internet über http://dnb.ddb.de abrufbar.

Table of Contents

List of Abbreviations

MC	*Midnight's Children*
MLS	*The Moor's Last Sigh*
SV	*The Satanic Verses*

1. Introduction

"A man who is beaten seriously ... will be irreversibly changed. His relationship to his own body, to his mind, to the world beyond himself alters in ways both subtle and overt", states Moraes Zogoiby, narrator and protagonist of Salman Rushdie's novel *The Moor's Last Sigh.* When he goes on to say that "beatings in different zones of the body affect different parts of the soul" and that "to be beaten for a long time upon the soles of the feet, for example, affects laughter", he draws on a connection that shall be a main concern of this paper (Rushdie, *MLS* 307). Moraes assumes that there is a link between a person's material body and his or her immaterial elements. A violation of the body is described as concerning more than a person's physical wholeness. The soul, the consciousness, and other components that are relevant for a person's self-definition are affected by the disruption of physical unity.

In Rushdie's writing, this connection between a person's body and a person's self is prevalent. While in the abovementioned quotation it is physical violence that points toward the complexity of this relationship, it can be seen as representative of a broader understanding of 'violent' experiences that threaten physical as well as psychological wholeness and thereby a person's sense of identity. In Salman Rushdie's work, the effects of history, migration and the difficulties present in a pluralist society such as India can be discussed in the context of identity.

How is identity formed? How is it disrupted? What is the function attributed to the body in the context of identity in Rushdie's writing? Brooks' assertion that in narrative "it is on the body itself that we look for the mark of identity" introduces the idea that shall be the focus of this paper (21). The questions connected to identity formation and crisis of identity will be analysed in respect to their connection to the body. However, it is not only the effects that a transformation or disruption of physical wholeness can have on the characters' identities that shall be addressed in this paper. The way identity crises can affect the characters' bodies will also be discussed. I shall consider three of Rushdie's novels, namely *Midnight's Children* (1981), *The Satanic Verses* (1988) and *The Moor's Last Sigh* (1995) to examine the processes at work in the formations of identity and the issues and challenges connected to them. These three novels have been chosen as they are each concerned with the theme of identity, a concept conveyed as being important in the protagonists' lives both in collective as well as in individual quests for wholeness and coherence. Furthermore, the novels, which have been considered a trilogy (cf. Rushdie, "The Moor's Last Sigh" 199) are connected thematically, a connection that is underlined by the fact that some characters 'migrate' from one story to the next.[1] Thus we encounter a character from *Midnight's Children*, Saleem's big-eared son Aadam, in *The Moor's Last Sigh*, just as the Indian art critic and doctor, Zeeny Vakil, from *The Satanic Verses* reappears in the successive novel. *The Moor's Last Sigh* can be regarded as a continuation of the plot of *Midnight's Children*, though narrated from an admittedly changed perspective.

First, I will attempt to give a brief overview of the approaches to the notion of identity in philosophy, sociology and psychology in order to offer a foundation for understanding the contemporary thinking on identity. While collective identities will be regarded as separate from personal identities, it is never intended to imply that both aspects are not intertwined. After expounding the contemporary thinking on the notion of identity, two (connected) phenomena that challenge the formations of identity are to be considered as they seem relevant for the later discussion of Rushdie's writing, namely decolonisation and (postcolonial) migration. While those are processes at work all over the world, when giving examples I shall restrict myself to India or Britain respectively, as those are the contexts most relevant for a discussion of Rushdie's earlier work. I will then proceed to outline the connection between body and identity in the fourth chapter. The admittedly important themes of gender and sexual identity[2] shall be neglected in the discussion of Rushdie's novels, as they would demand a separate discussion.

---

1 *Shame*, Rushdie's third novel, published in 1983, must be seen as being thematically affiliated with the other novels but shall be neglected, since for the purposes of this paper the findings would be similar to those resulting from an analysis of *Midnight's Children*.

2 An interesting aspect to be considered in this context could be, for instance, the fading and shrinking of men as opposed to women growing bigger and fatter (Reverend Mother - Aadam; Picture Singh - Durga (cf. *MC* 623); Hind - Muhammad Sufyan (cf. *SV*)). In *Shame*, the connection between political and gender oppression could be a prolific field of analysis.

In the following part, the focus will be on the main protagonist of each of the three novels as (literally) embodying a form of collective identity.[3] The chapter is divided into three subchapters, each of which primarily focuses on one novel while also referring to the other novels, where relevant. Next, the novels shall be regarded in the context of personal identity. With that, aspects such as genealogy, wholeness, and the continuity of identity will be the focus of the discussion. By discussing the power bodies can exert over selves, I shall show another facet of the link between body and self. In the last two chapters, I will then focus on the body and identity respectively: the body in its function as 'text' will be scrutinized, then an examination of the importance of narration and storytelling to the formation of identity will be discussed, while also alluding to the novels' metafictional elements.

---

3 The analysis of *The Satanic Verses* will mainly be restricted to the character of Saladin Chamcha, leaving Gibreel's dream sequences out entirely.

2. Concepts of Identity

The concept of identity has been the subject of discourse in a number of disciplines, especially in philosophy, sociology and psychology. Identity as defined in the *Oxford English Dictionary* is "the quality or condition of being the same in substance, composition, nature ... absolute or essential sameness, oneness", but also "the sameness of a person or thing at all times or in all circumstances; the condition or fact that a person or thing is itself and not something else; individuality, personality" ("Identity"). While the idea of identity as something that is defined by its stability is outdated and no more than an exploration of its semantic roots, this definition gives us an introduction to some of the key points that continue to be central to the identity debate, namely the notions of 'sameness', 'wholeness' and 'continuity'. The concept of identity has been a matter of discourse from the beginnings of philosophy and has, or at least the approach to it has, always undergone many changes. The current discourse about identity, especially in its contemporary problematic contexts, will be central to this summary.

When speaking about identity, one has to distinguish between personal and collective identities. Forms of collective identity can take shape as gender identity, ethnic or cultural, and national identity. Here, identity is, in its simplest terms, an individual's belonging to a certain group - a group with whose members the individual can feel 'identical' (cf. Assmann and Friese 12). The term 'personal identity' or 'self-identity', on the other hand, refers to individuals with reference only to themselves - a being identical to itself (cf. Wagner 45). According to Snow, "personal identities are the attributes and meanings attributed to oneself by the actor ... self-designations and self-attributions regarded as personally distinctive". While collective and personal identity will be considered separately in the following, their affiliation shall not be negated. Personal identity always has a social dimension to it as it is constructed in terms of the awareness of other people and relates to a meaningful orientation in a person's life that includes other individuals. Collective identity, on the other hand, can only emerge if several people direct the meaningful orientation of their personal identities towards the same collective (cf. Wagner 46). When a person embraces a collective identity, it usually means that it is "a highly salient part of their personal identity and sense of self" (Snow).

2.1 Personal Identity

One of the characteristics of modernity[4] is that it made the human being the centre of the world, 'the subject' (cf. Larrain 143). Originally, a person was seen as separated from historical and social dimensions and could thus be regarded as a coherent essence. The philosophical conception of identity was based on

> the belief in the existence of a self or inner core which emerges at birth, like a soul or essence, and which, in spite of being able to develop different potentialities in time, remains basically the same throughout life, thus providing a sense of continuity and self-recognition. (Larrain 144)

The prevalent question in philosophy and later in psychology and sociology connected with personal identity has been that of personal continuity. Personal identity, in this context, is the condition or fact of remaining the same person throughout various phases of existence (cf. "Identity"). John Locke was one of the first to give "the problem of personal identity its ... clearly identifiable formulation" in a chapter of his *Essay Concerning Human Understanding* (Noonan 24). The self as defined by John Locke is "that conscious thinking thing", which achieves stability through continuity of consciousness over time. The main point in Locke's theory on personal identity is that "consciousness makes personal identity" (Locke qtd. in Noonan 27). Locke thus defined identity in terms of memory: "it is memory alone that needs to be appealed to in providing a criterion of personal identity" (Noonan 9).[5] "And as far as this consciousness can be extended backwards to any past action or thought, so far reaches the identity of that person" (Locke qtd. in Noonan 33). The importance of the past is central to this understanding: one's present self and one's past self sharing knowledge of ac-

4 Modernity shall be understood in its relation to modernism and as an epoch in its context, the industrial age of the 19th century, preceding our present society, which can be understood as postmodernity.

5 Locke refers to the "experience-memory" and not factual memory or event-memory (Noonan 9).

tions in the past is what constitutes personal identity in Locke's view (cf. Noonan 43).

In social psychology and sociology, the idea of the subject as produced in social interaction became important (cf. Larrain 146). In modernity, the self or identity as something a person is born with was not unanimously rejected, but is rather accompanied by the approach that identity is a "construct and creation from available social roles and materials" (Kellner 233). That identity has entered into discussion and become problematic makes it more self-reflexive, personal and also "subject to change and innovation" (Kellner 231). Personal identity came to be seen as something that develops as a result of social experiences (cf. Larrain 146). In this context, George H. Mead introduced the possibility of a variety of selves: "there are all sorts of different selves answering to all sorts of different social reactions" (qtd. in Larrain 147). This quotation also illustrates how individual identity is necessarily part of social identity. However, it was still assumed that there is a complete self in a person's centre, which is coherent and consistent (cf. Larrain 147).

In modern society, the idea of the self was closely linked to individuality, to developing an individual and unique self (cf. Kellner 232). The autonomous subject, however, is fragmented in postmodernity "due to social processes which produce the levelling of individuality in a rationalized ... and consumerized mass society and media culture" (Kellner 233). The contemporary view of identity "accepts that identities are never unified and, in late modern times, increasingly fragmented and fractured; never singular but multiply constructed across different, often intersecting and antagonistic, discourses, practices and positions" (Hall, "Introduction" 4). Contemporary postmodern thought has "by and large rejected the essentialist and rationalist notion of identity and builds on the constructivist notion which it in turn problematizes" (Kellner 233). The contemporary concept of identity as outlined by theorist Stuart Hall "does *not* signal that stable core of the self, unfolding from beginning to end through all the vicissitudes of history without change; the bit of the self which remains always-already 'the same' identical to itself across time" (Hall, "Introduction" 3). On the contrary, the question of stability and instability, continuity and discontinuity, is one that accompanies the idea of identity more than ever. "Identity is never found by suspending the self in a mythical past, nor is it invented without a prehistory. Identity always oscillates between fixity and openness" (Papastergiadis 98). Although identity could be regarded as multiple or inconsistent in modernity, identities were yet relatively fixed as they derived from a set of roles or norms (cf. Kellner 231). While in earlier times, the issue was centred on the ways in which one could find and preserve a stable identity, nowadays identities are meant to be unstable and open (cf. Bauman 18). The heart of "post modern life strategy is not identity building, but avoidance of fixation" (Bauman 24). That is how Bauman comes to juxtapose the change in the understanding of identity from modernity to postmodernity in terms of an opposition of the pilgrim (who is "preoccupied with the daunting task of identity-building") to the tourist for whom identity has turned "from an asset into liability" (Bauman 24; 26). In postmodern theory, identities become more and more fragile. Even more so, postmodernist discourse questions the existence of identity *per se*. Some critics call the concept of identity as a whole a fiction (cf. Straub 98): "the discourses of postmodernity problematize the very notion of identity, claiming that it is myth and an illusion" (Kellner 233). According to Kellner, the modern self is aware of identity as being something that is constructed and that can be modified at will (cf. 232). Instead of talking about 'identity formation' it seems to be just as valid to talk about 'identity construction', as "the knowing subject is ... quite aware that [identities] are representations" and always constructed (Hall qtd. in Kennedy 5). The view that identity is the discovery of an innate essence, which determines a person's sense of self is rejected (cf. Kellner 233). Identity is not something that is simply 'there' and has to be found, but it is something that must be constructed and reconstructed (cf. Straub 93). Therefore, the quest for identity is not to be seen as a passive searching but an active making. This insight also leads to the view of identity as having a process-like nature: it is never final but always temporary and provisional. Straub describes identity as a unity that does not offer security and certainty, but as one that offers orientation in the social, moral and temporal space of possibilities in which a person lives (cf. 95).

Another aspect that shall be mentioned briefly in the context of postmodern culture is the blurring of boundaries. While, for instance, a blurring of the boundary between 'high' art and 'low' art is exemplary, also the private sphere "can no longer be analytically or symbolically separated from the public sphere" (Rojek qtd. in McGuigan 36). As society and culture become the subject of reorganization "the conventional distinction between public and private" is abolished (Dunn 105). Thereby, also the boundaries between self and other are problematized by "questioning the norms separating the public and the private" (Dunn 105).

2.2 Collective Identities

Collective identities are predominantly explored in sociology. There exists a plethora of collective or group identities, which might be based on nation, gender, class or ethnicity. While factors such as language, religion, ethnicity and especially place can be formative in a person's self-identity, they can also offer grounds for a form of collective identity. As has been established that an individual's personal identity might nowadays be seen as being potentially multiple and never final, a person can possess several social identities: being a Black Muslim, for instance, includes potentially at least two social identities.[6] When talking about collective identity we have to ask ourselves whether the concept as it was analysed in respect to personal identities can be transferred to the field of the collective. As we have seen, as soon as persons interact, they must designate themselves or each other respectively as social objects. This means that identities have to be assigned as a precondition for social interaction (cf. Snow). Collective identity implies the identification of individuals with each other, the formation of a group. In this sense, it might be embedded in existing social identities. Snow describes social identities as "orientation markers" which become, when activated, collective identities. An ethnic identity, for instance, might be 'there' just because a person's skin has a certain colour, but as soon as this person identifies with others sharing the same ethnic identity it becomes a salient one for the person – it is 'activated' as collective identity.

While 'personal identity' refers to a subject that is restricted by its corporality, 'collective identity' poses the question of the constitution of the collective (cf. Straub 98). That is where the shift in meaning takes place: from the identity of an individual to the unity of many. Theorists usually agree

---

6 Categorically based social identities and cultural identities will be understood as being part of the more general term 'collective identities' insofar as they all refer to a group identity. For a clearer distinction see Snow.

in a definition of collective identity as having its essence in a "shared sense of 'one-ness' or 'we-ness'" (Snow). The formation of a collective identity includes the assumption that this group is different from others. Hall describes identity formation as being part of a "play of specific modalities of power" as they are constructed through exclusion much more than through unity: "identities are constructed through ... difference" (4). Edward Said, in the "Afterword" to his seminal book *Orientalism* writes that

> the development and maintenance of every culture require the existence of another different and competing *alter ego*. The construction of identity - for identity, whether of Orient or Occident, France or Britain, while obviously a repository of collective experiences, is finally a construction - involves establishing opposites and others whose actuality is always subject to the continuous interpretation and re-interpretation of their differences from 'us'. Each age and society recreates its 'others'. Far from a static thing then, identity of self or of 'other' is a much worked-over historical, social, intellectual, and political process. (Said, Afterword 332)

The understanding of one's self in relation to the 'Other', the so-called "constitutive outside", is crucial to identity formation (Hall, "Introduction" 4): "the internal homogeneity which the term 'identity' treats as foundational is not a natural, but a constructed form of closure, every identity naming as its necessary, even if silenced and unspoken other, that which it 'lacks'" (Hall, "Introduction" 5). Although not necessarily to be understood as a negative concept, it is important to mention *Orientalism* in this context, in which Said demonstrates how Western societies 'othered' Eastern/'oriental' societies as a means of dealing with their 'otherness' and achieve their subordination. Said thus shows the extent to which the tendency towards 'exclusivism' in identity politics can become dangerous (cf. *Orientalism*).

Today, most theorists argue that 'identity pluralism' has dispelled ideas of mono-identities. Individuals are not usually seen as committing to one single idea anymore: "depending on the situation ... gender, regional, or national identities are stressed, revealed, activated, or suppressed and concealed" (Lützeler 3). These situationally specific identities do "not constitute a jumbled pile, but typically [form] an integrated, hierarchical structure; a social self" (Leik and Goulding 144). The description of identities as being covered and uncovered depending on the situation and thereby changing meaning, suggests the view of identities as palimpsestic. This assumption will be considered in the discussion of Rushdie's novels later in this paper.

3. Challenged Identities

The 20th century is defined by certain phenomena that pose challenges to the formation of individual as well as collective identities, which might be considered a crisis or welcomed as a challenge for the (collective) self. Globalization, decolonisation, and a society marked by rapid changes, are among the many factors that contribute to the discussion of identity discourse that marks our era. As has been established that identities are socially constructed and that they are "contingent on time, place, and social context", they must be fluid and unstable (Agnew 12).

3.1 Postcolonial Identity

The idea that identity is always constructed in relation to the 'other' or to what it lacks is especially relevant in postcolonial discourse. Colonisation deprives colonial subjects of great parts of their traditions, culture, their past - and thus identities. New traditions, different forms of education, administration and thereby new forms of identity are imposed on the colonised peoples. They become 'other', not just from the colonial perspective, but also as a consequence of the identity formation of the colonised subject, "who is forced into the internalisation of the self as an 'other'" (McLeod, *Beginning* 20; see also Fanon *Black Skin, White Masks*). Identities are defined in relation to colonial culture. However, under British rule in India for instance, most people could identify themselves as Indians while adopting parts of the British settler's culture. There was a feeling of national identity that was fed by the presence of the British, especially in the last decades of the British Raj, when the independence movement started. While "political jerrymandering of a heterogeneous people into nation-state identification" was attempted "for purposes of control and domination" (Radhakrishnan 753), it was exactly the processes of colonisation "of the Western world, that 'unified' these peoples across their differences in the same moment as it cut them off from direct access to their past" (Hall, "Cultural Identity" 227).[7] The existence of colonial rulers in India made it possible for the colonised to

[7] This quotation originally refers to the context of slavery but seems to be valid also for the consequences of colonialism.

identify themselves as a broader community against that presence. The vast process of decolonization after World War II not only posed questions for the people in terms of political reorganization, but especially with respect to a common identity that was not to be defined in terms of binary oppositions any longer. While the nationalist movement during the independence struggle in India showed Indians as united, this did not last, which becomes especially salient in India's partition into the states of India and Pakistan and the threat that communalism posed for unity after Independence (cf. Goonetilleke 27). It is important to remember that the act of decolonisation did not restore the ex-colonies to their former state. Although a political decolonisation took place, the processes of cultural decolonisation cannot be achieved as fast. Former colonised peoples cannot not simply go back to or recreate their old traditions, culture and identity. Colonisation "disfigures" and "destroys" or disrupts their past (Fanon qtd. in Hall, "Cultural Identity" 224) and colonial presence continues to be felt in terms of culture. In postcolonial identities, the 'power' that was the European dominance, has become a constitutive element (cf. Hall, "Cultural Identity" 233), and thus the time of colonisation remains formative in the consciousness of post-colonial nations as it initiated an anti-discourse (cf. Assmann 22).

> That imaginative distinction that differentiates between 'man' (self) with [sic] 'black man' (other) is an important, devastating part of the armoury of colonial domination, one that imprisons the mind as securely as chains imprison the body... . Colonialism is destroyed only once this way of thinking about identity is successfully challenged. (McLeod, *Beginning* 21)

It is significant to note that there is a 'dialogical negotiation' between constructed identities and the 'other' by which they are formed, meaning that postcolonial identities also influence the construction of the identities of former imperial nations (cf. Davies and Goh xiv). In *Maps of Englishness* Simon Gikandi depicts this connection by using the example of cricket. The game of cricket used to be seen as "an exclusively English creation unsullied by oriental ... influences", a game that stood for the core values of Englishness and a symbol of English culture (Sandiford qtd. in Gikandi 9). However, during the time of decolonisation and postcoloniality, the game acquired a different character: not only do former colonised people beat the English at the game nowadays, but the English had to adopt the new characteristics of the game that were established by the former colonised people. Thus, colonial categories such as cricket can be read "as the mark of the incomplete project of colonialism, as the institutions that allow formerly colonised peoples to hallow new spaces of identity and self-expression" (Gikandi 13). This example illustrates the ambiguity and two-sidedness of identity formation in the context of colonisation and stresses the fact that aspects of the colonised culture influence the colonisers and vice versa.

The term 'hybridity' has become important in the field of postcolonial discourse.[8] As a key concept when talking about postcolonial identities, it stresses the interdependence of the relation between colonisers and colonised in constructing their self-definitions. Coming from the field of biology, the term 'hybridity' means quite simply 'mixture'. In the 19th century discourses of scientific racism, it used to refer to "the negative consequences of racial encounters" (Papastergiadis 169). It alluded to the alleged contamination that the colonised might have brought upon the European colonisers, and was seen as "a threat to the fullness of selfhood" (Papastergiadis 168). Nowadays, however, the term has taken on a new meaning and found acceptance in cultural discourse. In the decolonisation era, hybridity refers to the struggle of postcolonial countries to form a new (national) identity under the ongoing influence of an imposed European identity. It can refer to linguistic, cultural, political as well as racial hybridization. It is an important concept in contemporary discourse in that it accepts identity as constructed through difference and that "the presence of fissures, gaps and contradictions is not necessarily a sign of failure" (Papastergiadis 170). It suggests that origins and influences are "multiple, complex and contradictory" and that thus our identity must be seen as hybrid (Papastergiadis 14). A hybrid is not considered a "physically weak, mentally inferior and morally confused" person anymore, but a "'bridging person', one that is both the benefactor of a cultural surplus, and the embodiment of a new synthesis" (Papastergiadis 15). There is an "ongoing process of differentiation and exchange" between cultures, thus hybridity serves as a metaphor for the "identity being produced from those conjunctions" (Song 2).

In the last years, the term has become associated especially with the work of Indian theorist Homi K. Bhabha. He argues that there is a 'third

[8] For criticism of the concept of hybridity as solving problems of identity politics see Hogan 526.

space' that is produced by the interaction of two cultures and marked by hybridity and fluidity. Here, intercultural contacts are not understood as dualistic but as taking place in the 'third space' in which the constitution of identity and alterity is seen as a mutual permeation of centre and periphery and oppressor and oppressed (cf. "Hybridität"). Hybridity has the potential to "reverse the structures of domination in the colonial situation" (Young qtd. in Ashcroft, Griffiths, and Tiffin, "Hybridity"):

> 'Bakhtin's intentional hybrid has been transformed by Bhabha into an active moment of challenge and resistance against a dominant colonial power… depriving the imposed imperialist culture, not only of the authority that it has for so long imposed politically ... but even of its own claims to authenticity. (Young qtd. in Ashcroft, Griffiths, and Tiffin, "Hybridity")

Moreover, the concept of mimicry has come to "describe the ambivalent relationship between colonizer and colonized" (Ashcroft, Griffiths, and Tiffin, "Mimicry"). It refers to colonial pressure to adopt the colonial ruler's habits, institutions and values. It is

> the desire for a reformed, recognizable Other, as *a subject of a difference that is almost the same, but not quite.* Which is to say, that the discourse of mimicry is constructed around an *ambivalence;* in order to be effective, mimicry must continually produce its slippage, its excess, its difference (Bhabha, "Of Mimicry and Man" 126).

Therefore, "the effect of mimicry on the authority of colonial discourse is profound and disturbing" (Bhabha, "Of Mimicry and Man" 126). As the result of mimicry can never be an exact copy, it is always potentially mockery. Thereby mimicry becomes resemblance as well as menace: "[t]he *menace* of mimicry is its *double* vision which in disclosing the ambivalence of colonial discourse also disrupts its authority" (Bhabha, "Of Mimicry and Man" 129). It "reveals the limitation in the authority of colonial discourse" (Ashcroft, Griffiths, and Tiffin, "Mimicry").

Hybridity as the "creation of new transcultural forms" has been described within the contact zone of colonization (Ashcroft, Griffiths, and Tiffin, "Hybridity" 118). Yet also outside the context of postcolonial studies, the term 'hybridity' has become "one of the most useful concepts for representing the meaning of cultural difference in identity" (Papastergiadis 14). It can also refer to the assumption that a person's self-identity in this world must always be incomplete as it is formed by interaction with others and can therefore only be an ongoing process (cf. Papastergiadis 14–15).

Hall describes two possible ways of thinking about cultural identity: the first one implies that cultural identity means having "one shared culture, a sort of collective 'one true self', hiding inside the many other, more superficial or artificially imposed 'selves'" (Hall, "Cultural Identity" 223).[9] In this sense, our cultural identity would reflect common historical experiences, which provide us "with stable, unchanging, continuous frames of reference and meaning" (223). Hall sees the rediscovery of this identity the object of "passionate research" especially in post-colonial societies (Fanon qtd. in Hall, "Cultural Identity" 223). Quoting Frantz Fanon, Hall asks whether it is really only a matter of 'digging up' the continuities of the past that were suppressed by colonial experience or whether this 'research' should be seen as a production of identity (cf. 224). He stresses that histories can offer a way to impose an "imaginary coherence on the experience of dispersal and fragmentation" that colonised societies or diasporic peoples suffered. However, instead of seeing identity as an "already accomplished fact" he tends to regard it as a "production" (222). Thus, in the second view of cultural identity, the emphasis is on the "points of deep and significant difference which constitute 'what we really are'" as one "cannot speak for very long, with any exactness, about 'one experience, one identity', without acknowledging its ... discontinuities" (225). This is why we should see (cultural) identity not only as belonging to the past, but also as belonging to the future and as undergoing "constant transformation" (225). While "the role of the past is a significant force on the shaping of any identity, it does not have the exclusive power to determine all the possibilities for shaping identity in the present" (Papastergiadis 14). This is how Hall would like to understand the 'colonial experience'. In the formation of cultural identity, two processes are going on simultaneously: there is a dialogic relationship between "the vector of similarity and continuity; and the vector of difference and rupture" (226).

---

9 Unless indicated otherwise, the following citations in this subchapter refer to Stuart Hall's article "Cultural Identity and Diaspora".

3.2 The Migrant's Identity

Globalization and migration constitute an important background when considering the more recent discourse about identity. Although it is hardly a new phenomenon, in the 20th century migration has taken place on a bigger scale than ever before. Hall regards the processes of globalization as being coterminous with modernity ("Introduction" 4), and Papastergiadis calls it "a metaphor for the complex forces which are integral to the radical transformations of modernity" (2). Generally, it is seen as having added to a change in the character of populations and cultures. In terms of identity, migration can add to the feeling of uncertainty and fluidity which has already been singled out as a feature of contemporary society, and which can prompt or magnify forms of identity crises.

Nations used to be an important referent in the discussion of collective identity formation and have seemed to present a stable principle. Nation-building has been an attempt to unite diverse peoples in a common identity. Today, however, we can speak of de-territorialized identities, as the boundaries of a nation-state are no guarantor of a common identity any longer. Individuals may construct their identities around concepts such as religion, language or cultural practices, which are not restricted to a particular territory anymore (cf. Papastergiadis 84). Movement across territorial borders has contributed to "destabilize the foundations of the nation-state" and can thus add to the uncertainty of the notion of belonging (Papastergiadis 2). Cultural identities that define the sense of belonging in terms of national categories have to be questioned in times, which have seen the emergence of new forms of identities, namely diasporic and hybrid identities (Papastergiadis 2). As we understand the notions of place and roots as an essential component in the processes of personal as well as collective identity formation, migration has to be viewed not only as a geographical and physical displacement, but also as a psychological one. As Sanga points out, "migration is a phenomenon that involves a transfer of peoples and, along with them, their social, cultural, and political ideologies. Thus migration is a displacement or a disruption that affects the total identity of a person" (5). Salman Rushdie considers the image of the migrant as "the defining image of the 20th Century" and migration as an important indication of the methods of a person's self-definition:

> If you look at the 19th Century definition of the self, for example, three of the most important things in that definition are the idea of the roots, of belonging to a particular place, of the self as defined in place in a landscape: the figure in a landscape; the idea of community, of habits, of custom, of fellowship, as being part of the self. And the idea of language ... What happens in migration classically is that you lose all three – you no longer belong to a place; you no longer belong to a language; you no longer belong to any kind of broad community. You have to start again. But this means there is a sort of disruption in the idea of the self. (Rushdie, "Interview at San Francisco" 77)

This understanding of migration as disruption clarifies that "the re-negotiating of identities is fundamental to migration" (Davies 3). Our world is marked by a process of commingling that takes place as an outcome of the meeting of cultures. Social identities, like all forms of identity, are neither pure nor static, but rather "change in new circumstances or by sharing social space with other heritages and influences" (May, Modood, and Squires 8). The migrant must build an identity that is "hyphenated, ... the migrant constructs an identity that is established by and dependent on different cultural systems" (Sanga 5). This challenges not only the migrant's identity but also existing conceptions of host-identities, with an effect that can be described as similar to that of mutual hybridization as described above. Migrants' identities do not have an exclusive origin, but owe something to the "stream of life" of the host society and thereby must contribute something to it, too (Modood 78):

> The identity of the citizen presupposes the other, the migrant, the exile. Identity emerges, not just from the identification of the common characteristics for those who are included in the nation, but from the more visible differences of those excluded. The national question: 'Who are we?' is largely answered by declaring: 'We are not them.' (Papastergiadis 59)

Here, we must talk of 'hybrid identities' once again, to describe "what is neither indigenous nor exogenous" in the sense in which Bhabha uses the term: hybridity emerges through "constant change and adaptation and from being marginalized" – processes that take place in migration (Agnew 12). Diasporic experiences are defined "not by essence or purity, but by the recognition of a necessary heterogeneity and diversity; by a conception of identity which lives with and through, not despite difference; by hybridity" (Hall, "Cultural Identity" 235).

The "concern with place and displacement" emerged as a central theme particularly in postcolonial literatures (Ashcroft, Griffiths, and Tiffin, *Empire* 8). Bhabha suggests that "where once the transmission of national traditions was the major theme of a world literature", now "transnational histories of migrants, the colonized, or political refugees – these border and frontier conditions – may be the terrains of world literature" (Bhabha, "Introduction" 12).

4. Body and Identity

Theories and literature concerned with identity have continually shown an interest in the connection between a person's body and self-identity. In Greek philosophy, the quality of the connection between mind and body was widely discussed. While ideas varied, major philosophers such as Socrates, Plato and Aristotle agreed that there is a 'built-in conflict' between body and soul and that the soul is superior to the body (Synnott 9). Descartes' dualism, which considers the body as being from the material world and thus separate from the soul, has been seminal in this context. The division within the self "coincided and reflected the division within society" - the soul was attributed to church, the body to science (Synnott 23). Descartes, who saw the mind as the home of reason and called the body a machine concluded that the mind is the only criterion for personal identity and considered the body as inferior (cf. Manecke 7). Naturally this view has been subsequently attacked: some thinkers insisted on a unity and equality of body and mind (Spinoza, later Freud) or even reversed the assumption that the mind is superior to the body (Nietzsche). Sartre saw the body as the self when he wrote "I am my body to the extent that I am" (qtd. in Synnott 32). However, the Cartesian mind-body dualism has continued to be central to most discussions.

In contemporary society, individuals seem to define themselves more and more by means of their bodies, seeing them as constitutive of the self (cf. Shilling 158). The body as the "'visible carrier' of the self" plays a key role in a person's self-identity (Best 158). By being worked on and reconstructed, the body loses its meaning as a "given, an aspect of nature" and becomes an "'outer layer' through which the reflexive project of the self" enters (Giddens 218). The body *appears* to be a solid basis on which one can build a reliable self-identity (cf. Shilling 158), but has "become an inadequate basis on which the project of the self can be built", not least because in high modernity the meaning of the body itself has been called into question (Shilling 158). Moreover, Michel Foucault has asserted that "nothing in man - not even his body - is sufficiently stable to serve as a basis for self-recognition or for understanding other men" (qtd. in Hall, "Introduction" 11). Stuart Hall sees the body as serving the function of a "signifier of the condensation of subjectivities in the individual" ("Introduction" 11). However he does not consider the body to be a stable referent; at the same time, the body's function as a signifier does not necessarily depend on its stability as a referent in the first place (cf. Hall, "Introduction" 11).

Our bodies are not only physical entities but have a cultural and social dimension to them: "the body is not just skin and bones, an assemblage of parts, a medical marvel ... The body is also, and primarily, the self. We are all embodied" (Synnott 1). This can mean quite simply, that, for instance, the colour of our skin determines parts of our social identities or that our sex determines our gender identity[10]. The body is the first external determinant through which we are seen in society. Thus, personal identity does not only depend on how we see ourselves, but is also connected to our social identity - which is, in turn, constituted by how we are seen by others. The body consequently becomes "the meeting point between private and public" (Taylor 105).

Our own perception of our body seems to be important to our feeling of 'wholeness'. This becomes clear when looking at unsound bodies; illness can indeed destabilise identity (cf. Straub 95). In sociological discourse, illness is often seen as a threat to the integrity of the self; as disrupting "a sense of wholeness of body and self" (Charmaz 657). "The healthy body parallels the mind, but when sickness strikes, the essential nature of the body is exposed" (Kirmayer qtd. in Lupton 87).

Nancy Scheper-Hughes and Margaret Lock see the body as "inseparable from society, both as symbolic and as political" (Synnott 235). In their article "The Mindful Body" they claim that the "individual body should be seen as the most immediate, the proximate terrain where social truths and social contradictions are played out, as well as a locus of personal and social resistance, creativity and struggle" (31). The body as a model, which can stand for "any bounded system", has been used as an image not only in private but also in public spheres (Douglas qtd. in Synnott 229). From classical antiquity to the 17th century, "somatic figures for society, its constituent members, and its operations" were widely employed (Harris 1). The phrase 'body politic' drew a comparison between the human body and the human society in order to illustrate the unity of the state or society. The

10 Also gender identities, however, have become more fluid (see Best 158).

macrocosm of the state was analysed and discussed in terms of its microcosmic equivalent, the organic system of the human body. The correspondence between the physical body and the body politic has offered ground for stylistic usage of the organic system as metaphor especially in political and philosophical thought, as well as in religious rhetoric. The idea of a corrupt society as a diseased body was particularly prevalent (cf. Hale 20–22). While the political use of the analogy originated in Greek city-states, an early version can be traced in the Indian *Rig-Veda*, where we find a description of the creation of the castes from Purusa's body (cf. Hale 24).[11] Similarly, in the *Mahabharata*, one of the two most important Sanskrit epics from ancient India (the other being the *Ramayana*), a debate between the mind and the organs is used to show how humans should interact in society ("Analogy"). Furthermore, what comes to mind in the context of the body as an image for society is Thomas Hobbes' *Leviathan*: the king as a sovereign whose body is made up of many individual bodies, to show the idea that "the sovereign is the head of a body composed of his subjects and that all spiritual and temporal power is gathered in his hands" (Hale 128). The structure of the state is described in terms of body parts in Hobbes: the sovereign is the soul of the commonwealth, public ministers are the organs (cf. Hale 128). The body politic can be seen as an "artificial body" which "men gave birth to" (Pateman qtd. in Kortenaar 131). Nowadays, however, the metaphor of the body politic is seen as a dead phrase, which is simply synonymous with 'the state' or 'nation' (cf. Hale 131; Harris 1). As Kortenaar points out, while Hobbes' imagery shows that only the sovereign could embody the whole, nowadays individuals expand their selves to the scale of the nation, as "we all say, more or less, with Louis XIV: *L'État, c'est moi!*" (Balzac qtd. in Kortenaar 131), implying the centrality of the self.

Foucault defined the body as an organisational principle, "employed in modern societies whereby docile and productive citizens were fashioned from otherwise impulsive and unruly individuals" (Mills and Sen 1). Thus,

---

11 When they divided Purusa how many portions did they make?

...

The Brahman [priests] was his mouth, of both his arms
was the Rajanya [warriors] made.
His thighs became the Vaisya [shepherds], from his
feet the Sudra [servants] was produced. (qtd. in Hale 24)

he saw the body as "central to ... the processes of modern society" (Mills and Sen 1). It has also been an important subject in colonial and postcolonial discourse. Theorists such as Said argued that the body was "the central trope of colonial discourses that constructed difference between the West and the non-West" (Mills and Sen 1). The non-Western body was seen as weak and inferior whereas the Western body was idealized. This led historians and cultural critics to regard the body as being at the centre of the justification for colonialism (cf. Mills and Sen 2). Theorists have identified that the construction of otherness within a colonial context often depends on corporeal criteria (cf. Keown 24), as "early concerns with the body centred on ideas of colour and race" (Ashcroft, Griffiths, and Tiffin, "Postcolonial Body").

The understanding of the body varies from culture to culture and is therefore "eminently social" (Synnott 37). In Indian thought, such as Hindu religion, philosophy, literature, and Indian culture generally, the body is essential to the understanding of the Indian self (cf. Dissanayake 39). While Indian philosophical or religious traditions cannot be seen as forming a single homogenous entity, they share some common features concerning body and mind/self. The body is regarded as a living mechanism that "integrates a complex variety of mental and physical processes", meaning that "the human body is a body-mind rather than a mere body or a body to which a mind is somehow attached" (Koller 45). The body is considered an ongoing process that never reaches completion. At the moment of death, the "inner self discards the body and finds home in another one" (Dissanayake 40). Koller points out that Indian philosophers were different from their Western counterparts in that they did not draw a dividing line between body and mind but saw the mental and the physical as "aspects of an integrated process, seeing the body as conscious and consciousness as bodily activity" (47). Therefore, "from the Indian perspective, body is never rejected in favor of mind as the authentic self" (Koller 47). Apart from Buddhism and Carvaka, all traditions view the body-mind as embodying the Self. Nevertheless, the nature of body-mind and its relation to the self is problematic.[12] In Indian tradition, the issue is not how to relate body and mind, but to re-

---

12 Both body and mind are rejected as the authentic self of a person. For further information see Thomas P. Kasulis, Roger T. Aimes, and Wimal Dissanayake's *Self as Body in Asian Theory and Practice*.

late 'Self' and body-mind to each other (Koller 47). "The Self is considered to be transcendent and independent of the body-mind complex ... while the body-mind has both physical and mental characteristics, the Self transcends both the physical and the mental" (Miura 104).

Joseph S. Alter attributes a public function to the body in contemporary Indian society. He states that "there is a great deal of concern among various groups with the relationship between health, identity and the moral integrity of both the nation as a whole and the citizenry who constitute that whole" (16). Alter explains how men train and rebuild their bodies so as to rebuild the nation in the context of the Indian wrestling culture (cf. 17). Here, the body is ascribed more than metaphorical meaning: it reflects collective identities. This example advises us of the connection between public and private, between nation and individual bodies. Also Melissa Butcher sees the body as a central signifier in Indian society:

> The body is a central icon of Indian identity in its progression through the 20th century – it has encapsulated visions of economic and cultural Indianness (Gandhi); of discipline and pain (castrated, jailed...); and of global India (Miss World). It has been enscribed [sic] upon throughout the 50 years of Indian Independence, from a symbol of freedom, to that of discipline and restraint, to freedom once more in the form of market choice and liberalization... . it is a site of coherence and persistence but also a marker of cultural transition ... . The body is then transformed into a representation of the meanings and the social organisation of the cultural space within which it is embedded. (240)

The functions of the body and its link to identity shall be further explored in the context of Salman Rushdie's fiction.

4.1 Body and Identity in Literature

The body offers a wide range of metaphorical possibilities. Organic analogies were, as we have seen, widely employed in political writing and rhetoric but can also be consistently found in literary writing. While the analogy of the body politic seems to have died out, the phrase continues to be used especially in comparisons that make use of the image of disease or infection. The transforming body in particular, most often changing due to illness or disease, has been a constant device in popular as well as in 'high brow' literature. The function of the image of the body is not restricted to comparisons and analogies to the state. It can inhere the purpose of revealing the psychological development of the characters; illness can thus serve as a "test of the moral fibre of the afflicted individual or society, exposing their true nature" and disease as "a recurrent metaphor for moral or social decay" as well as "a vision of collective social disaster" (Lutpton 51). In writings concerned with colonialism or its aftermath, we can detect a "metaphoric link between the diseased colonized body and the depredations of colonialism" (Keown 131). Postcolonial writers might represent dysfunctional bodies as a metaphor for political corruption (cf. Keown 28). The body in modern literature is therefore "a site of signification – the place for the inscriptions of stories – and itself a signifier, a prime agent in narrative plot and meaning" (Brooks qtd. in Ball 127).

A striking example of a concern with the question of the homogeneity of body and self dates back to the Roman poet Ovid. In literature, the most important illustration may be his narrative poem *Metamorphoses,* which is preoccupied with just that theme. Telling of "bodies changed to other forms" (Ovid I.1), the poem "deals with extreme vicissitudes of the human body and with the accompanying emotions" (Hardie 41). In an Ovidian universe that is in constant flux, only souls remain unchanged. The poem engages in a depiction of the "feelings of a person being imprisoned within a body that is not what he or she essentially is" (Montserrat 82). In *The Satanic Verses,* the Ovidian standpoint is opposed to that of Lucretius, who sees "the considerations about the soul's ability to be affected by bodily changes" (Warren 30) to prove that the soul is corporeal and mortal and "perish[es] at last and one with the body" (Lucretius 3.754).

The importance of the *Metamorphoses* becomes even more apparent when taking stock of the number of writers who were influenced by Ovid's poem. In the context of this paper it will prove relevant, too, as "metamorphosis is a defining dynamic of certain kinds of stories – myths and wonder tales, fairy stories and magic realist novels" (Warner 18).

5. Public Spheres and Privates Bodies: Embodied Identities in Salman Rushdie's *Midnight's Children*, *The Satanic Verses* and *The Moor's Last Sigh*

As mentioned above, the question of identity is a major theme in postcolonial and postmodern literatures, features of both of which are to be traced in Rushdie's fiction. In the following chapter, the body shall be scrutinized as a site upon which identities, "social truths and social contradictions are played out" (Scheper-Hughes and Lock 31). In the three novels under discussion we are confronted with situations connected to India's colonial past or Britain's imperial past respectively, namely struggles India met after achieving Independence, issues connected to postcolonial migration, as well as the challenges of a pluralist society in a postcolonial state. As each of the novels' protagonists finds himself in a society dealing with these situations, it shall be shown how they are to be seen as embodiments of such complex conditions.

5.1 Preliminary Remarks on Style and Form

While it is not easy to define Magic Realism as a genre and Rushdie cannot be classified as a magic realist writer *per se*, it is commonly acknowledged that he incorporates themes typical of magic realism while also experimenting with its effects and techniques (cf. "Magic Realism"). In her essay on the 'genre', Faris talks about a "particular kind of verbal magic" that the reader experiences in magic realist writing (176). In this respect, an important aspect to consider when analysing Rushdie's fiction is his use of metaphors. Evidently, Rushdie's writing is rich with physical imagery. A special device is the kind of imagery in which a psychological state manifests itself physically: an invented disease becomes real (*MLS* 210), the "pessimism of Picture Singh expand[s]" until it seemingly becomes a "physical entity" (Rushdie, *MC* 630), flowers bleed real blood (*MC* 187), "the dreadful allergy of desire" is the cause of inflammation and itches (*MLS* 93), and an "old maid's bile" is sewn into clothes (*MC* 214). These are only a few examples of Rushdie's "linguistic magic", which "happens when a metaphor is made real" (Faris 176). By literalising metaphors, the "dichotomy realistic language = true/rhetorical language = false" can be overturned (Linguanti 6–7).

Feelings or emotions become not only physical entities, but also physical symptoms: Amina's feeling of guilt about meeting her ex-husband (and about gambling) becomes a visible cloud and expresses itself on her body in the form of verrucas (*MC* 218). How the body becomes the centre of conflicts in the critical processes of identity formation will be shown in the following part of this paper.

For Rushdie, "magic realism ... expresses a genuinely 'Third World' consciousness" (qtd. in Petersson 45). In his novels, "it is the Westerner, who becomes 'other'. Magic, which in the colonial novel often functions as the sign of the otherness of non-Western society and civilization, with Rushdie becomes daily reality, ... indigenous magic" (D'Haen 198). The literalisation of metaphor is an important device in Rushdie's writing. Saleem, narrator and protagonist in *Midnight's Children*, writes that "reality can have metaphorical content", however, "that does not make it less real" (*MC* 278). In the following, it shall be shown how this metaphorical content is to be considered as enhancing the clarity of our understanding of reality (cf. Merivale 338). The "exploration of the metaphorical properties of the human body as a medium for exploring the dynamics" at work in the postcolonial society of independent India as well as in 'multicultural' Britain will be considered in particular (Keown 16).

According to Frederic Jameson,

> [a]ll third-world texts are necessarily ... allegorical, and in a very specific way: they are to be read as what I will call national allegories, even when, or perhaps I should say, particularly when their forms develop out of predominantly western machineries of representation, such as the novel... . Third-world texts, even those which are seemingly private and invested with a properly libidinal dynamic necessarily project a political dimension in the form of national allegory: *the story of the private individual destiny is always an allegory of the embattled situation of the public third-world culture and society.* [13] (69, emphasis in original)

13 This model has been exhaustively critiqued for its homogenization of colonial experiences and its replication of colonialism's center/periphery organization (see Schultheis 573–574). The extent to which Jameson's assumption falls short in the context of *Midnight's Children* will be referred to in the course of this paper.

Therefore Rushdie's novels must be seen as (trans)national allegories. The interconnectedness of these two aspects, allegory and literalised bodily metaphors, shall be described as 'embodiment'.[14] While Saleem Sinai's fictional autobiography *Midnight's Children*, which directly addresses the problems of post-independence India, has become a famous example of that, *The Satanic Verses* and *The Moor's Last Sigh* can also be read along these lines.

5.2 Body as National Allegory

While Saleem Sinai, born at the exact moment of Indian Independence, shall be the main concern of this section, it will also prove interesting to consider other characters as 'embodiments'. The novel starts about thirty years before Independence in Kashmir, with the story of Aadam Sinai, Saleem's grandfather. He can be seen as one part of a binary pair: Aadam, 'westernized' after returning from Germany where he received medical training, stands for progress and modernity. He is opposed to the boatman Tai, who can be seen as standing for tradition and history: "nobody could remember when Tai had been young" (*MC* 10); his body is "ancient" (*MC* 12). He is seen as "the living antithesis of [the Western] belief in the inevitability of change" (*MC* 11). His decision to stop washing himself is described as "a gesture of unchangingness" (*MC* 29). Tai's retrogressive attitude is underlined by his refusal to wash his body; he comes to literally embody changelessness and the refusal to let go of the past by accumulating it, in the guise of dirt and bad smells on his body.

As Patrick C. Hogan points out, another pre-independence embodiment can be found in Saleem's grandmother Naseem, later referred to as Reverend Mother, a name that seems to recall 'Mother India' (529). As Aadam regards her through the holes of a perforated sheet, he comes to see one

---

14 The theme of embodied identities can also be seen on a non-allegorical level. Ayesha, a character we encounter in one of Gibreel's dream sequences, is an example of that. She claims she can speak to the archangel. Her being "possessed by the demon of epilepsy" (*SV* 221) identifies her as a 'chosen one' as epilepsy was seen as "both a sign of human sinfulness and as a sign of sacred election" (Turner 89). Similarly, the seer who gives Amina a prophecy before Saleem's birth in *Midnight's Children* "suddenly [falls] to the floor and froth[s] at the mouth" (*MC* 115). By attributing characters a physical defect, they are *identified*; a certain characteristic is ascribed to them.

body part at a time. He is described as being haunted by the phantasm of a "partitioned woman" (*MC* 26), the term partitioned indicating a link with the nation (cf. Hogan 529). However, the picture of the whole he forms in his mind is not more than "a badly-fitting collage of her severally-inspected parts" (*MC* 26). According to Hogan, "Aadam's partial and discontinuous views of Naseem mirrors anyone's partial and discontinuous view of a nation, for our experience of a nation is necessarily an experience of bits and pieces only; we do not sense the whole directly, but imagine it" (529). Aadam loves Naseem in fragments, however, when she is "unified and transmuted into the formidable figure she would always remain" his love for her fades (*MC* 47).

5.2.1 *Birth of the Nation*

> At the stroke of the midnight hour, when the world sleeps, India will awake to life and freedom. A moment comes, which comes but rarely in history, when we step out from the old to the new, when an age ends, and when the soul of a nation, long suppressed, finds utterance... . Freedom and power bring responsibility. The responsibility rests upon this Assembly, a sovereign body representing the sovereign people of India. Before the birth of freedom we have endured the pains of labour and our hearts are heavy with the memory of this sorrow. Some of those pains continue even now. Nevertheless, the past is over and it is future that beckons us now. (Nehru 1)

Jawaharlal Nehru, Independent India's first Prime Minister, compared the process of becoming independent to that of giving birth. Gandhi spoke of a "vivisection of his motherland", referring to the separation of India and Pakistan while Nehru, eventually accepting partition, thought that by "cutting off the head we will get rid of the headache" (qtd. in Zachariah 137). As mentioned before, bodily metaphors have a long tradition in military and political oratory, thereby linking a matter belonging to the private domain to the public sphere. Depictions of the body politic as an organic system can be found in Rushdie's writing as well. In *Midnight's Children,* the population of India is described as a many-headed monster whose blood is replaced with "corpuscles of saffron and green" at the hour of Independence, midnight, on the 15th of August in 1947 (*MC* 154). By making Saleem's body an image of India and India's common identity after the end of the Raj, Rushdie expands the metaphor. Jameson's assumption that "the story of the private individual destiny is ... an allegory of the embattled situation of the public" is, as we shall see, to a certain extent true for *Midnight's Children* (69).

Even before his birth Saleem becomes public property; the countdown to the moment of birth is paralleled with a countdown to the proclamation of India's Independence (cf. *MC* 100). Rushdie has taken Nehru's birth-metaphor literally "by adding the pangs and screams, the forceps and midwives" (Kortenaar 34). The (fictional) letter Rushdie's Nehru writes to Saleem Sinai condemns the latter to a life in which private matters become public and public matters become private. Having been born at the exact hour of Independence, he is "the newest bearer of the ancient face of India which is also eternally young" (*MC* 167). Saleem's life, writes a fictional Nehru, "will be, in a sense, the mirror of our own" (*MC* 167). Thus "handcuffed to history" Saleem's life, as well as his body, come to represent the state of India (*MC* 586).

Saleem himself draws attention to the fact that his own life is to be seen as a national allegory. *Midnight's Children* withstands Jameson's claim that even "seemingly private" novels are to be seen as national allegories in that it never claims to be private. As if anticipating Jameson, Saleem fills in for potential critics in a metafictional fashion, when pondering on his own assertion of his fate being connected to that of India[15]:

> How, in what terms, may the career of a single individual be said to impinge on the fate of a nation? I must answer in adverbs and hyphens: I was linked to history both literally and metaphorically, both actively and passively, in what our (admirably modern) scientists might term 'modes of connection' composed of dualistically-combined configurations of the two pairs of opposed adverbs given above. (*MC* 330)

His connection to his home country is a mutual one: Saleem's actions have an influence on the nation, just as the nation's turmoil influences Saleem's fate. This fact is paralleled by the depiction of the body, which becomes "the meeting point between private and public" (Taylor 105). The nose receives special attention as it is described as the "place where the outside world meets the world inside" (*MC* 15). "If they don't get on, you feel it

---

15 Rushdie voices his view on allegory in general and allegorical elements in *Midnight's Children* in "*Midnight's Children* and *Shame*".

here", Tai warns Saleem's grandfather Aadam as a boy, foreshadowing the importance and many meanings of noses in the Aziz family as well as the potential for conflict that goes along with a connection between public and private matters (*MC* 15).

Aadam Aziz "introduces the corporate, somatic basis of Indian identity" in the very beginning of the novel (Kane 95), when the three drops of blood falling from his nose become diamonds (cf. *MC* 4). Furthermore, Aadam represents the dynamics of Indian identity: before he witnesses the Jallianwala Bagh Massacre of 1919 Aadam feels Kashmiri, not Indian, and "Kashmir, after all, is not strictly speaking a part of the Empire, but an independent princely state" (*MC* 38). However, the brutality of what he sees during the massacre, in which more than four hundred unarmed Indian protestors were shot as a British brigadier ordered his troops to fire on the crowd (cf. Guha 569), changes Aadam: "I started off as a Kashmiri ... [t]hen I got a bruise on the chest that turned me into an Indian" (*MC* 47). A similar assertion can be found in *The Moor's Last Sigh*, where Moraes, narrator and protagonist, states how the political situation influences his family's sense of belonging to a group identity: "Before the Emergency we were Indians. After we were Christian Jews" (*MLS* 235). The experience of colonial violence leads to the identification with a national identity, while the experience of the Indian Emergency seems to lead to further division between minorities. The change in Aadam's feeling of identity is accompanied by a physical marker: when he falls down in the chaos of the massacre's violence, his doctor's bag presses on his chest and inflicts "upon it a bruise so severe and mysterious that it will not fade until after his death" (*MC* 41), a bruise in which to find "the answer to the question, Indian or Kashmiri?" (*MC* 143). The massacre provoked collective outrage which was "skilfully used by Mahatma Gandhi to launch a countrywide campaign against colonial rule" (Guha 569). It remains important as an event that prompted many Indians to turn against the British and thus unite them by a national identity.

After Saleem's birth and therefore after Independence, colonialism is still present in India. His family lives in the former residence of departing Englishman William Methwold, which they buy a few weeks before Independence on the condition that they leave the house unchanged until the legal end of British rule. Even after Methwold's departure, however, the cocktail hour that was introduced by him remains a regular part of their afternoons.[16] By living in this English house, among the relicts of the British Raj, Saleem's family is changed (cf. *MC* 131). Saleem's description of how his father's voice alters, how "in the presence of the Englishman it ... become[s] a hideous mockery of an Oxford drawl" (*MC* 127), can be connected to Homi Bhabha's concept of mimicry. Saleem himself states that "it would be fair to say that Europe repeats itself, in India, as farce" (*MC* 256). On the one hand, Ahmed Sinai's imitation that turns into mockery reminds the Indians of their failure to become authentically British and of the continuation of their colonial status. On the other hand, it can be regarded as a reminder of colonialism's *partial* success. In India the colonial enforcement of mimicry was laid out in Macaulay's notorious "Minute on Education" of 1835, which aimed at creating "a class of persons Indian in blood and colour, but English in tastes, in opinions, in morals and in intellect" who were to function as "interpreters between [the British] and the millions whom [the British] govern" (qtd. in Rocher 256).[17] The goal was, as Charles Grant put it, to provide the colonial with "a sense of identity as [the British] know it" (qtd. in Bhabha "Of Mimicry and Man" 127).[18] However, the colonial's body continued to serve as a means of distinguishing colonised and coloniser: mimicry was to produce people that were "almost the same, *but not quite*", or, as clearly indicated in Macaulay, "almost the same but not white" (Bhabha, "Of Mimicry and Man" 126; 130).

Frantz Fanon writes in *The Wretched of the Earth* that the postcolonial native bourgeoisie were in compliance with the motto "replace the foreigners" (Fanon 105). In *Midnight's Children*, Saleem's family seems to exemplify that phenomenon. Not only the continued cocktail hour can be seen in this context but also the "pigmentation disorder" that affects Ahmed Sinai, Saleem's father, as well as a large number of Indian businessmen: he "was a late victim of a widespread, though generally unremarked phenomenon" (*MC* 248). As they profit from the Five Year Plan, "the businessmen of India [are] turning white" (*MC* 248). Secretly, Ahmed Sinai is even pleased with

---

16 The cocktail hour seems to be an assertion of the continuing negative effect of colonialism in that it is the implied reason for Ahmed's alcoholism.

17 This passage is also quoted in *The Moor's Last Sigh* (cf. 376).

18 Charles Grant was Chairman of the East India Company and wrote "Observations on the State of Society among young Asiatic Subjects of Great Britain" in 1792.

that development, as he "has long envied Europeans their pigmentation" (*MC* 247). He has become partly anglicised in his 'opinions and tastes' and now he is being 'Europeanised' in his physique. His function is not to serve as an interpreter any longer but to replace the British. Here, Rushdie invents an 'Epochenkrankheit': the disease pattern has not only physiological, but cultural causes (cf. Degler and Kohlroß 15).

However, as Kortenaar points out, William Methwold's "Englishness is no less mimic than that of the people who take over the Estate": a fact which is symbolised in the description of Methwold's hair (169). When Methwold leaves the Estate to return to England, it is revealed that his hair, his centre-parting, which is the residing place of his power, is only a wig (cf. *MC* 153). This points to a recent development in postcolonial studies: the concept of mimicry is not only applied to natives, but in some degree to the colonisers themselves.

The pigmentation disorder highlights the importance of skin to the definition of social identity. Amina, Saleem's mother, is segregated in her family because of her dark "skin of a South Indian fisherwoman" (*MC* 69). For women in India in particular, fair skin is a desirable quality, while having dark skin is a "proof of your inferiority" as "even blackies know white is nicer" (*MC* 89–90). Rushdie satirises this attitude when he has Zohra, Ahmed Sinai's cousin, pay Amina a compliment by calling her as black as "a white lady standing in the shade" (*MC* 90). The whitening of the Indians' skin is described as "a disease which leaked into history and erupted on an enormous scale shortly after Independence" (*MC* 53) and is explained as being a symbol of the "the outward expression of the internationalism of ... spirit" (*MC* 54). Skin (and the colour of one's skin), having been an important marker during colonial times, stays meaningful and becomes a symbol of the characters' attitude towards postcolonial India. The Indian businessmen, who are affected by the 'disorder', are profiting from the processes of decolonisation after all. The notion that skin is an outward expression of spirit or soul can also be found in *The Satanic Verses*: Gibreel, as his "archangelic other self", can see "the decay of the souls blistering and bubbling on the skins of people in the street" (320). The symbolic importance of skin shall be taken up again in the discussion of *The Moor's Last Sigh* at a later point in this paper.

An interesting episode has Saleem telling the reader about his "first mutilation" (*MC* 318). The half-English (bastard) teacher named Zagallo humiliates Saleem by comparing his face to the map of India. Eventually, he tears some of Saleem's hair out. After that, Zagallo does not come back to Saleem's school, so that the latter is led to think it is because his "uprooted hair ... stuck to [Zagallo's] hands, like bloodstains that wouldn't wash out" (*MC* 322). The hair on the teacher's hand being compared to bloodstains is to be read as a reference to Macbeth, a hint made obvious by a classmate's comment that "the first sign of madness are bloodstains" and "the second sign is looking for them" (*MC* 322). The student's apparently sound knowledge of Macbeth, as well as the fact that the headmaster of Saleem's school is called Mr Crusoe, "like Robinson" (*MC* 326), point to the fact that the educational system has not yet been adapted to the processes of decolonisation and that the student-teacher relationship is still preconditioned by the colonial past. However, Zagallo makes it very obvious that he despises his "jungle-Indian" students and wants to draw a line between their status and his own, as he himself is a mimic man (*MC* 318). Therefore, that Zagallo does not return after the fateful day of mutilation as "no one wants a teacher with hair on his palms" points to the interpretation that Saleem thinks his hair has 'stained' the teacher (*MC* 322).

5.2.2 Growing Up

In Saleem's description of himself as a child it becomes evident that he sees himself as sharing his fate with that of the Indian state. When in his mother's womb, "many-headed monsters swell inside" him, these monsters representing the Indian population (cf. *MC* 145). His body must be seen as consisting of every Indian: "All part of the luggage I brought into the world ... do you wonder, then, that I was a heavy child" (*MC* 146). Saleem "swallow[s] the world" not only metaphorically but literally, as he becomes heavy with the weight of the Indian population (*MC* 146.). Once he is born, Saleem grows fast, almost magically so. He himself calls it a "heroic programme of self-enlargement" as if he knew that to "carry the burdens of [his] future life, [he]'d need to be pretty big" (*MC* 169). The parallel to the nation is patent: India grows bigger, almost day by day, as over five hundred formerly autonomous chiefdoms are dissolved into fourteen new administrative units of India (cf. Guha 44). Later, when Saleem is eleven, his growth is not compared to India's size anymore, but to the "accelerated history" of that year (*MC* 334). These are the correlations that Saleem terms his "passively-metaphorical" connection to India (*MC* 330).

The circumstance that Saleem, as a baby, does not close his eyelids can also be seen as a case in point. According to Calasso, "only what is conscious blinks" (qtd. in Kortenaar 99) – therefore Saleem's inability to blink shows he has not formed a self yet. His ayah Mary and his mother *train* him to blink, asserting "control over a sign of consciousness that is so natural as to be unconscious" (Kortenaar 99), thereby teaching him "the first lesson of [his] life: nobody can face the world with his eyes open all the time" (*MC* 171).

After the first months of Saleem's life, as well as India's first months as an independent nation, "as if incapable of assimilating so many goings-on", Saleem is infected with typhoid (*MC* 203). This might be seen as reflecting the "threat of disintegration" that was very real in India at that time, as some of the bigger princely states seemed unwilling to join the union (Guha 57). An Englishman quoted in Guha's *India After Gandhi* wrote in 1947 that after India's division into India and Pakistan, India seemed unstable. He wonders whether the division will stop there, or whether the subcontinent will "break up into innumerable, small, warring States" (57). When the political issues are solved and Saleem survives, thanks to Dr Shaapsteker's snake venene, his "growth-rate lost its phenomenal aspects" (*MC* 204).

Rushdie himself, as well as numerous critics, have named several intertexts relevant to *Midnight's Children*. For the idea of embodiment in general, but especially in respect to the character of Saleem, Günter Grass' *The Tin Drum* is important. The fact that Oskar Matzerath decides to stop growing can be seen as a literalised metaphor operating similarly to Rushdie's. Like Oskar with his glass-shattering voice and special gift for drumming, Saleem possesses special powers. During the "accident in the washing chest" Saleem's nose gives way to that "world-altering ... irreversible *sniff*" (*MC* 223), which makes something in his sinuses burst. This is the beginning of his gift of telepathy, his "nose beg[ins] to sing" and re-emphasises its importance as a link between the public and the private (*MC* 224). His gift lets him enter the mind and seemingly the body of any Indian: "I was inside him, tasting the warmth as he gurgled down a frothing glass of urine" (*MC* 241). Saleem feels like the bodies he "occupie[s] act at [his] demand" (*MC*

241). His gift becomes greater by means of another accident: colliding with his friend Sonny in a bicycle accident, Saleem's "bulging temples found their way into Sonny's hollows. A perfect fit. Heads fitting together" (*MC* 259). After that, not only can he visit the head of any Indian but he can communicate and act as a forum, a "national network", for the other midnight's children, born like him in the first hour of Independence (*MC* 314). They are a "vast gallery of grotesques and human curiosities who stand for the truly infinite human variety of the Indian subcontinent" (Brigg 180). Uprety points to the significance of their miraculous gifts as illustrating "the moment of maximum hybridity", at which they are born (373). The moment of Independence is a "temporal space that is traced by an interweaving of different symbolic systems" (Uprety 373). To Saleem, the children of midnight are "a sort of many-headed monster", "the very essence of plurality" (*MC* 317), but, paradoxically, he "gives the children a *homogenous* quality, as 'multiplicity' simply means the variety of the children's special midnight-given powers" (Strand 999). Acknowledging their vast metaphorical possibilities, Saleem states that although the "midnight's children can be made to represent many things ... what they must not become is the bizarre creation of a rambling diseased mind. No: illness is neither here nor there" (*MC* 278). They not only represent the multitude of the Indian subcontinent but they come to symbolise an "auspicious national destiny" (Brennan 82). As the "hope of freedom", they can be seen as an embodiment of the optimism disease, which has broken out already several years before Independence (*MC* 278). Saleem's formation of the Midnight's Children Conference, his attempt to bring the children of midnight together in a democratic body, equals the attempt at uniting different people within the frame of one nation; it "represents the dream of romantic nationalism" (Kane 100). In Saleem's formation of the MCC, a longing for national form marked by unity, equality and democracy is revealed. However, the attempt to unite all the different people of India, rich and poor, Hindu and Muslim, is bound to fail, in spite of Saleem's warning to "not permit the endless duality of ... them-and-us" to threaten the dream of a united India (*MC* 354). Saleem "goes on to indicate that categorical identity reifies us, reduces our ongoing, multiple, unfixable selfhood to mere objects. He protests in vain that 'people are not things'" (Hogan 523). However, as India starts to fragment further "cracks in the Conference" appear (*MC* 353). The motif of fragmentation and disintegration is prevalent in *Midnight's Children*. The perforated sheet is its prime symbol. When Saleem's grandfather falls in love with his grandmother, he can only see her through a hole in a perforated sheet. He forms a picture "of Naseem in his mind, a badly-fitting collage of her severally-inspected parts" (*MC* 26). "Here Naseem, India, is imagined as a whole, ... [as] South Asia in its entirety. She is dreamed of as a whole that will be partitioned. In contrast, Saleem represents India after 1947. It would make no sense to speak of him as being partitioned. He is one result of partition" (Hogan 530).

This 'habit' to love in fragments is passed down to Amina Sinai, who, having failed to fall in love with him at once, "resolve[s] to fall in love with her husband bit by bit" by selecting a different fragment of her husband each day (*MC* 87). India becomes fragmented herself, firstly due to the partition into Pakistan and India. Fragmentation does not stop there: in 1956, "India [is] divided anew, into fourteen states and six centrally administered territories. The boundaries of these states were ... walls of words. Language divided us" (*MC* 261). India's fragmentation becomes a physical one: after the 1957 election, India's 'body' disintegrates, as roads crack open in the heat (*MC* 310).

All these fragmentations are to be seen as foreshadowing, or rather presupposing, Saleem's own physical disintegration. Saleem is furious when a doctor pronounces him whole in spite of his cracks. As the doctor calls his cracking up imaginary, Saleem ensures the reader that it is not less real because it is metaphorical (*MC* 83).[19] For Saleem, this shows how people choose to believe in an imaginary wholeness. India is indeed seen as a "collective dream" rather than a united nation (*MC* 150). "In all the thousands of years of Indian history, there never was such a creature as a united India", writes Rushdie in "The Riddle of Midnight" (27). Thus even after Independence, India remains a country divided by language, race, religion and culture. Therefore Saleem, containing the multitudes that constitute India, is sure that he "shall eventually crumble into (approximately) six hundred and thirty million particles", the population of India at the time (*MC* 43). His disintegration "becomes a metonymy for that of the national

---

[19] Kane has read this episode as indicating that clinical medicine is blind to the ex-colonial's pain as it relies on an "alien" standard of interpretation (99).

collage as a whole, a country that looks whole on the map but that has ... become increasingly divided from itself" (Gorra 114–115).

5.2.3 Emergency

> We felt that the country has developed a disease and, if it is to be cured soon, it has to be given a dose of medicine even if it is a bitter dose. However dear a child may be, if the doctor has prescribed bitter pills for him, they have to be administered for his cure ... So we gave this bitter pill to the nation. (Indira Gandhi qtd. in Guha 495)

The birth of the new independent nation in the beginning of the novel is paralleled by Saleem's birth. In a similar way, yet another historical milestone is mirrored in a birth: the declaration of Emergency by Indira Gandhi: "the birth of Aadam Sinai ... found a mirror in the events of the night of the 25th of June" (*MC* 581). When Indira Gandhi is "found guilty of campaign malpractice ... Parvati enters labour", and when Parvati is giving birth, so is Indira Gandhi, "to a child of her own" - Emergency Rule (*MC* 582–585). Aadam has to fight a disease shortly after his birth, reflecting the turmoil India went through during the Emergency. In contrast to Saleem years earlier, "Aadam, wrestling with the serpents of disease, scarcely grew at all" (*MC* 593). Aadam contracts tuberculosis, which, as Saleem believes is "not unconnected with the larger, macrocosmic disease, under whose influence the sun had become as pallid as and diseased as [his] son" (*MC* 590). Saleem is convinced that, as long as the state of emergency lasts in India, Aadam will not get better. Aadam is determined to remain silent (cf. *MC* 590), thereby, as Uma Parameswaran points out, paralleling "the nation's silent acceptance of the new dictatorship" (qtd. in Smale 69). While Saleem is convinced that Aadam's illness is to be interpreted metaphorically, Parvati, Aadam's mother, sees his silence as the source of his illness and gives him a powder to release the "long-suppressed sounds of his babyhood" (*MC* 591). Playing on the colour of (independent) India's flag, Rushdie has Aadam turn "first saffron, then saffron-and-green, and finally the colour of grass" from the suppressed sounds that should be the outcry of the nation (*MC* 591). Saleem finds confirmation in his diagnosis as his son gets better after the fall of the 'Widow' (cf. *MC* 622).

Aadam, like Saleem before him, belongs to a whole new generation, the "Emergency-born" (MC 594), identified by a belly-button that sticks out instead of in, rather than by miraculous gifts like the children of midnight (cf. *MC* 626). Whereas Saleem tried to face the world with his eyes open all the time in the first weeks of his life, Aadam, in contrast prefers to keep his eyes firmly closed. Waiting silently, Aadam's special gift seems to be "to listen and wait until the new generation of children can rise" (Brigg 179).

However, if Aadam embodies the state in Emergency, Indira Gandhi herself is drawn on for physical metaphors as well. Hair, a decisive trait in the character of Methwold, is given special attention once again. Both Methwold and Gandhi are figures that symbolize oppression and power (cf. Goonetilleke 34), and, just as Methwold's power is said to reside in his hair, Gandhi's centre parting is shown as meaningful: "[S]he had white hair on one side and black on the other; the Emergency, too, had a white part – public, visible, documented, a matter for historians – and a black part, which, being secret macabre untold, must be a matter for us" (*MC* 588). Saleem goes as far as to say that Gandhi's hair does not only reflect the two sides of Emergency Rule but that it presupposes it: "[I]f the Mother of the Nation had had a coiffure of uniform pigment, the Emergency she spawned might easily have lacked a darker side" (*MC* 588). The effect that a physical feature, even a seemingly superficial feature, might have on history is carried to extremes here and points to the absurdity of Saleem's own claims on an active-literal influence on the nation. Indira Gandhi tries to create another identity during the Emergency, an identity between the authoritarian ruler and the nation: "India is Indira and Indira is India" (*MC* 587). That makes Saleem and 'the Widow' "competitors for centrality" (*MC* 587). Saleem's infection with "the Indian disease, this urge to encapsulate the whole of reality" (*MC* 97), has become evident throughout the novel, in particular when he claims that the "the hidden purpose of the Indo-Pakistani war of 1965 was nothing more nor less than the elimination of my benighted family from the face of the earth" (*MC* 469). When Indira Gandhi's slogan renders her an embodiment of the nation, Saleem sees her "lust for centrality" as the reason for what is to come (*MC* 587).

The violation of physical wholeness that occurred during the time of Emergency is an important aspect connecting the body and national consciousness. Violence took place in the form of numerous arrests but foremost in the context of a birth control programme, which led to many voluntary but many forced sterilisations. In Rushdie's novel, the castrations performed on the midnight's children depict how the violation of the body leads to more than a distorted sense of bodily identity. Vasectomy becomes more than a medical act, it becomes a "sperectomy: the draining out of hope" (*MC* 611). Looking back at the introductory quotation from *The Moor's Last Sigh*, physical violence is described in a similar way. A beaten man loses more than physical wholeness, "a certain confidence, a certain liberty is beaten out for good", while "often, what is beaten in is detachment" (*MLS* 307). Liberty as well as hope become entities that are 'removed' from the body by the impact of violence. The effects of the sterilisations (or, in the case of the children of midnight, the castrations) go beyond the ones to be expected from a medical point of view. By removing organs from their bodies, the doctors remove something from their souls, parts of their identity. In this way, the "optimism disease" that characterized generations of Indians, is finally defeated (*MC* 616). In *Midnight's Children*, this seems to be the 'bitter pill' that can cure India in Gandhi's eyes. After having been drained "above" during the operation on his sinuses and having lost his ability to communicate with the other children of midnight, Saleem is now also drained "below" - subsequently, he is "no longer connected to history" (*MC* 617):

> Because in drainage lie the origins of the cracks: my hapless, pulverized body, drained above and below, began to crack because it was dried out. Parched, it yielded at last to the effects of a lifetime's battering. And now there is rip tear crunch, and a stench issuing through the fissures, which must be the smell of death. (*MC* 645)

As 'hope', the only unifying element is exorcised, Saleem's vision of complete disintegration comes true. "[S]plitting breaking beneath the awful pressure of the crowd, bag of bones falling down down down ... a broken creature spilling pieces of itself into the street", Saleem becomes a 'human bomb' and cracks up completely (*MC* 647).

5.3 Body as Trans-National Allegory: the Migrant's Experience

If Saleem is seen as embodying the post-Independence Indian state, his sister, too, becomes an embodiment. Her family's emigration to Pakistan seems to be a metamorphic experience for her. A former tomboy, the Brass Monkey is transformed into Jamila Singer (a new name that goes along with a new identity); she veils her face and comes to be seen as the personification of the 'land of the pure' (cf. Goonetilleke, cf. *MC* 435). As her grandmother before her, she is placed behind a perforated sheet. However, the holes in the sheet do not seem to indicate partition, "the blank sheet or veil, pure and white, that stands in place of Jamila's body reflects back the unity of the nation" (Heffernan 483). The effect the migratory experience has on Saleem is less reconciliatory. Saleem's perceived confinement becomes a symptom as his "second period of hurtling growth" comes to an end in Pakistan (*MC* 394). More importantly, "somehow the existence of a frontier 'jammed' [his] thought-transmissions to the more-than-five-hundred" - Saleem is geographically and physically exiled from his fellow children of midnight; the geographical border impedes their mental communication (*MC* 394), thereby illustrating the psychological consequences of migration.

In *The Satanic Verses*, Gibreel, who shall later be regarded in his embodiment of a migrant's attitude, is regarded as the personification of India before he leaves for England. When he, a celebrated Bollywood star, gets sick and has the public worry about his life, the question the Indian people ask themselves is: "If Gibreel died, could India be far behind?" (Rushdie, *SV* 29). Once Gibreel recovers, a national holiday is declared, making of Gibreel's body, which already 'belongs' to the Indian public due to his profession, a symbol of India. Another important aspect in this episode, namely the effect of Gibreel's loss of religious identity that seems to have triggered his mysterious disease, shall be considered at a later point in this paper.

The theme of migrancy is an aspect widely explored in postcolonial literature, and in terms of discussions of collective identity it is the major concern of *The Satanic Verses*. In Rushdie's writings, we are asked to consider migrancy in more than a literal sense. It can be understood as a "metaphor for the complex forces which are integral to the radical transformations of modernity" (Papastergiadis 2). While these transformations question the way we understand our sense of belonging in a very personal manner, they also shed light on the processes of identity formation at work in a multicultural society. One of the main contexts in which Rushdie addresses the subject of the migrant's experience in *The Satanic Verses* is that of metamorphosis. According to Rushdie, "pressures exerted by migration are one of the classic contemporary locations of metamorphosis ... a carrying across of the self into another place and another language" (Rushdie, "Between God and Devil" 95). The change of place is connected to a loss of history: "all migrants leave their pasts behind ... it is the fate of the immigrants to be stripped of history" (Rushdie, *Shame* 63). In *The Moor's Last Sigh* we find a description of the implications of migration when Moraes Zogoiby travels to Spain: "The place, language, people and customs I knew had all been removed from me by the simple act of boarding this flying vehicle; and these, for most of us, are the four anchors of the soul" (*MLS* 383). *The Satanic Verses* starts in medias res with the main characters, Gibreel Farishta and Saladin Chamcha, falling out of the sky from an exploding airplane and landing on British ground - an opening describing the "most dramatic act of immigration" one can imagine (Rushdie, "Salman Rushdie" 128). As soon as they touch English soil, the two men start metamorphosing: Chamcha grows horns and Gibreel has light streaming softly outwards from behind his head (cf. *SV* 142). The narrator informs the reader that he should not be surprised by these "mutations", as they are to be expected as a price to be paid for being reborn (*SV* 133). Rebirth, in Hindu belief, is the ultimate form of metamorphosis (and migration), the soul being reborn in another body.

Chamcha subsequently becomes the "'borderline' figure of a massive historical displacement" - namely postcolonial migration (Bhabha, "How Newness Enters" 224). After 'the fall', he is suspected to be an illegal immigrant and deported. He is maltreated and abused by the policemen, which, to his confusion, seems to have nothing to do with his transformation "into a supernatural imp" (*SV* 158). As bewildering as this circumstance seems to him, the immigration officers treat him "as if it were the most banal and familiar matter they could imagine" (*SV* 158). And indeed it turns out it must be a familiar sight for them. That is to say, Chamcha is not the only disfigured migrant we encounter in the novel. He is brought to a sanatorium where he finds out his transformation is far from unique. He meets a woman who is "mostly water-buffalo" and hears about businessmen who have grown tails and African tourists who have turned into snakes (*SV* 168). How did these metamorphoses come about? "They describe us", Chamcha is told, "they have the power of description, and we succumb to the pictures they construct" (*SV* 168). The immigrants Chamcha comes across in the sanatorium are "demonized by the 'host culture's' attitude to them" (Rushdie, "In Good Faith" 402). Their transformations must thus be regarded as images of their identities as seen by the English. Images that are translated into actual physical form: Chamcha's dark, hairy appearance that is a result of his transformation corresponds to British racial stereotypes about Indians, as does the constantly "sizeable erection emerging from his loins" (*SV* 291). In *Orientalism*, Edward Said "showed how the Orient became a mirror in which Europe saw its own reflection, revealing both its objective but also its imagined differences from the Orient" (Kennedy 3). Said's view that writing and representation played an important role in processes of colonisation and racist attitudes is echoed in the explanation Saladin receives from his fellow sanatorium inmate. We can speak of a form of linguistic domination: "This is an important, indeed crucial, point, echoing the idea which Linda Hutcheon has described as that which postmodernism problematises: the connections between the linguistic and the political, the rhetorical and the repressive" (Kuortti 146). In writing *The Satanic Verses*, Rushdie can be said to 'reclaim' the "power of description" for the immigrant community while postulating hybridity and heterogeneity, which makes them agents in the construction of British identity (cf. Stein 182).

Along these lines, the sanatorium also reflects British identity insofar as it is defined in contrast to the migrants'. We can view Chamcha's metamorphosis as a counter-image of the way the British see their own identity. Chamcha's devilish form gives us insight into their fears and the way they see themselves in contrast to the 'other'. Chamcha becomes what Stuart Hall terms the "constitutive outside" (Hall, "Introduction" 4).

While the transformations occurring in *The Satanic Verses* remind the reader of Ovid's *Metmorphoses*, an interesting intertext in this context is also Lucius Apuleius' *Golden Ass*. It is directly referred to in the "Apuleian sympathy" Sufyan offers to Chamcha and the hope of reversing his transformation (*SV* 244). In *The Golden* Ass, the protagonist's metamorphosis into a donkey is not permanent and presents a way to make him see the world through different eyes whilst receiving a moral lesson. While Apuleius examines the condition of the lower classes, Rushdie writes his novel as "a migrant's-eye view of the world", including the racist attitudes of the host society (Rushdie, "In Good Faith" 394). One main purpose of the metamorphoses is thus to convey social criticism. As Walker remarks, "in magical realist terms, metamorphosis is as common an event as racist stereotyping is in terms of traditional social realism" (351). The point Rushdie arguably manages to make here is that "Britain is undergoing the critical phase of its postcolonial period. The crisis is not simply economic or political. It is a crisis of the whole culture, of the society's entire sense of itself" (Rushdie qtd. in Brennan 149). Rushdie emphasises the graveness of the situation when saying that the immigrant community is to the British

> a new community of subject peoples of whom they can think, and with whom they can deal, in very much the same way as their predecessors thought of and dealt with 'the fluttered folk and wild', the 'new-caught sullen peoples, half devil and half-child' (Rushdie, "Empire").

Punday writes about Shelley's *Frankenstein* that "bringing together many different elements of the culture in the monster's body for the sake of revealing problems within the society itself" is the stuff of very effective cultural critique (806); this is certainly valid for Saladin Chamcha's monstrosity. Chamcha becomes a symbol of difference in British culture as a "kind of third term that problematizes the clash of extremes" (Cohen qtd. in Punday 806). Saladin grasps the nature of the situation in one of his dreams, in which he relives the escape from the sanatorium with the physiotherapist Hyacinth, a migrant like himself. The closer they get to central London, the more extreme the change of their physique:

> [A]s captivity receded and the city drew nearer, Hyacinth's face and body had seemed to change. He saw the gap opening and widening between her central upper incisors, and the way her hair knotted and plaited itself into medusas, and the strange triangularity of her profile ... He saw in the yellow light that her skin was growing darker by the minute, and her teeth more prominent, and her body as long as a child's stick-figure drawing. (*SV* 254)

When Muhammad Sufyan offers Chamcha a place to stay "among your own people, your own kind" (*SV* 253), Chamcha feels appalled at the thought of belonging to that community. For him, being regarded as an illegal immigrant or even belonging to the Black community in London is agonizing, as he has been striving to get away from 'his own kind' most of his life, trying instead to be 'more British than the British' since he was a boy. Strikingly, as he realises that he has physically become the "embodiment of wrong, of what-we-hate, of sin" (*SV* 256), Saladin uses the first person plural, "what-*we*-hate", thereby clearly placing himself on the British side of the 'us'/'them' dichotomy. He admits that he cannot consider Mishal and Anahita, daughters of the Bangladeshi immigrant Sufyan, as "really" British "in any way he could recognize" although they have lived in Britain their whole life and regard themselves as British (*SV* 259). This attitude confirms what his devilish appearance reveals: immigrants are considered in terms of their origins and not in terms of what they might have become; thus 'even' someone like Saladin is bound to be seen as a devilish creature.

His first metamorphosis, that of "Salahuddin Chamchawala into Saladin Chamcha" or that journey from "Indianness to Englishness, an immeasurable distance" (*SV* 41), began years before, when he still lived in Bombay and supported the English and not the Indian cricket team (*SV* 37). By "pray[ing] for an England victory ... for the proper order of things to be maintained" (*SV* 37), Chamcha passes the 'Tebbit test' and thus proves that he is 'worthy' of being considered truly English even before becoming a British citizen.[20] In England, he falls in love with Pamela Lovelace, who, to him represents the epitome of an English upper class woman, and realises that successfully wooing her means fully completing his metamorphosis. He consciously *creates* an English self and rejects his other Indian self (*SV* 50).

Instead of 'hyphenating' his identity, Chamcha tries to get rid of everything that is Indian about him. His attitude towards British culture is hinted at in his name. Chamcha means 'spoon' and "point[s] to intimacy and, indeed, complicity between the authority of colonialism and its colonial subjects ... relations that continue in the postcolonial context" (Brennan qtd. in Smale 89). In Rushdie's own words, a 'chamcha' is "a person who sucks up to powerful people, a yes-man, a sycophant ... You could say that the Empire grew fat by being spoon-fed" (Rushdie, "Empire"). Chamcha even finds himself dreaming of a physical union with Britain, of "making tender love to the Monarch. She was the body of Britain, the avatar of the State,

---

20 The phrase 'Tebbit Test' refers to a proposition by Norman Tebbit, a British conservative politician, from 1990 (two years after the publication of *The Satanic Verses*). He controversially suggested that people from ethnic minorities should not be considered truly British unless they support the England cricket team instead of the team of their birth country.

and he had chosen her, joined with her; she was his Beloved, the moon of his delight" (*SV* 169). Similar to what the term 'chamcha' implies, the figure of the mimic is "hybrid inasmuch that he or she reflects or appears to adopt the qualities and values of colonial authority" (qtd. in Smale 98). Saladin Chamcha is driven by the desire "to become authentic: authentically British perhaps, although ... this could always slide into being more British than the British" (Huddart 65). Chamcha's metamorphosis can be interpreted as a result of mimicry that "backfired on him" (Sanga 36). According to Bhabha, true imitation is in fact never possible and is always potential mockery. Chamcha's transformation is mockery insofar as it shows the "hollowness that lies at the core of national identities" (Sanga 37). Chamcha's view of England is that of a "picture postcard"; he attempts to establish his English identity by means of adopting cultural patterns (cf. Stein 182). For him, England seems to consist of "cricket, the Houses of Parliament, the Queen" (*SV* 175). In *Midnight's Children* we encounter a comparable figure in the blind landowner who claims to enjoy European paintings without being able to see them. Like Saladin Chamcha, he accepts colonial culture (and therefore indirectly power) without questioning it (cf. *MC* 21).

The metamorphosis that transforms Chamcha also draws attention to the discrepancy between his self-perception and the way other people perceive him. Being maltreated by the immigration officers, he thinks that "this isn't England" (*SV* 158), it is certainly not the "picture postcard" England always was to him (*SV* 175). Zeeny, the Indian woman he has an affair with in Bombay, tries to open his eyes about why he is a voice impersonator rather than an actor: "They pay you to imitate them, as long as they don't have to look at you. Your voice becomes famous but they hide your face" (*SV* 60). Her idea is confirmed by the nickname "Brown Uncle Tom" that Chamcha goes by in Britain (*SV* 267). Zeeny calls his loving the British in spite of their racist attitudes a "slave mentality" (*SV* 61). This corresponds to what Rushdie calls "imaginary homelands"; migrants are forced to "make a new imaginative relationship with the world" (Rushdie, "Location of Brazil" 125).

Saladin's metamorphosis is also an expression of the way his physical identity is connected to his social identity: by changing physically he becomes further alienated from the way he saw himself; he becomes 'one of them' which renders his efforts to construct a British identity utterly futile.

As Chamcha, however, is not the only immigrant we encounter, it is worth taking a look at Chamcha's host Muhammad Sufyan and his family, who came to England after Sufyan's involvement in communist activities back in Bangladesh. In this case it is interesting to consider the role of the body: back in Bangladesh, Hind, Sufyan's wife, had gained a lot of weight, as she had tried to parallel her husband's "pluralistic openness of mind" by cooking food "from the multiple cultures of the subcontinent" (*SV* 245). She began to get fat as "all that food had to find a home somewhere, and she began to resemble the wide rolling land mass itself, the subcontinent without frontiers, because food passes across any boundary you may care to mention" (*SV* 246). Her "gastronomic pluralism" makes her "body alter" and become fat (*SV* 247). Her husband Muhammad Sufyan, however, who "swallowed the multiple cultures of the subcontinent", including the Western culture that became part of the subcontinent's heritage, gained no weight; he "refus[ed] to fatten" (*SV* 246). It is enlightening to connect this episode with an issue Rushdie raises in the context of migrancy: "What does it mean to be an 'Indian' outside India? How can culture be preserved without becoming ossified? ... What are the consequences of embracing those ideas and practices and turning away from the ones that came with us?" (Rushdie qtd. in Smale 88). Hind's consumption of the subcontinent's food can be seen as an attempt to preserve that culture within her body. She and her husband represent two different kinds of migrants' attitudes: Hind becomes the subcontinent herself, culture becomes ossified. Sufyan, on the other hand, is not only gastronomically but spiritually pluralistic. By 'refusing' to get fat he not only insults Hind's cooking, he also differs from her general attitude, which is that of an exiled person. Sufyan does not suffer from the separation from his home country, and, as if to prove it, "even [begins] to put on weight, fattening up in Proper London as he had never done back home" (*SV* 249). In this context the two Hinds in the novel can be likened to one another. Hind, the wife of the city council of Jahilia, the city of Gibreel's dreams, represents unchangingness as her body does not age (*SV* 360).

As Chamcha lives in Sufyan's bed and breakfast, he continues to change form, the main change being that he continues to grow. On the one hand, this is an intensification of his ongoing metamorphosis, on the other hand it symbolises the growth of his presence in the younger Asian immigrant community (cf. *SV* 285). Saladin, in his devilish form, first starts appearing to them in their dreams, and very quickly, the "image of the dream-devil start[s] catching on" until he is "everywhere" (*SV* 286). While for the police the plastic devil-horns young Asians wear on their heads justify the way they treat the immigrants, for the Black community, the "Goatman" provides an image of collective identification. As Sufyan's daughter Mishal explains: "It's an image white society has rejected for so long that we can really take it, you know, occupy it, inhabit it, reclaim it and make it our own" (*SV* 287). In the chapter entitled "Mahound", further insight into that 'strategy' is provided: "To turn insults into strengths, whigs, tories, Blacks all chose to wear with pride the names they were given in scorn" (*SV* 93). By "reclaiming language from [their] opponents" the Asian kids proudly wear rubber devil-horns as an "assertion of pride in identity" (Rushdie, "In Good Faith" 403). This also points to the "novel's exploration of morality as internal and shifting (rather than external, divinely sanctioned, absolute)" (Rushdie, "In Good Faith" 403). In The Hot Wax club, a nightspot where young people from immigrant communities meet, "named, no doubt, after Sufyan's translation of Ovid's waxy metaphor for the immutability of the migrant soul" (Bhabha, "How Newness Enters" 228), the separation of society is illustrated by means of wax figures. Figures of former migrants and slaves are juxtaposed with those of Thatcher and other figures standing for racist attitudes. By melting the latter in a nightly ritual, the Black communities take revenge and vent their anger as they melt icons of Englishness into formlessness (cf. *SV* 292–293).

While Gibreel's inner division is rooted in a spiritual crisis rather than in his migration to England, he also embodies a migrant's attitude. The ontological difference between him and Chamcha becomes apparent in the very beginning of the novel when, falling from the sky, Gibreel sings the Indian song "Oh, my shoes are Japanese...my heart's Indian for all that" while Chamcha sings "Rule, Britannia" (*SV* 5–6). In Chamcha, we find a migrant who is trying to assimilate so desperately that he eventually belongs nowhere, being called a devil by his Indian father as well as by the British, while in Gibreel we encounter a migrant who dislikes the host culture and, instead of assimilating to it, is resolved to change it. He represents the "avenging migrant" (Bhabha, "Dissemination" 169):

> These powerless English! – Did they not think their history would return to haunt them? – 'The native is an oppressed person whose permanent dream is to become the persecutor' (Fanon)... He would make this land anew. He was the Archangel, Gibreel. (*SV* 353)

Starting by changing "that most naturalised sign of cultural difference", the weather, Gibreel decides to transform the English (Bhabha qtd. in Smale 101). This transformation occurs as a very physical process: the "forces of the transformational process rushed out of his body (for was he not their *embodiment*?)" (*SV* 355). Contrary to Saladin, "although Gibreel is clearly transformed in many ways by his experience, this change remains primarily psychological" (Punday 813). As Walker points out, Gibreel is "not in the situation of Fanon's colonial native, but rather in a more complex post-colonial situation, to which the native's dream of becoming the persecutor no longer corresponds" (357). Therefore, Gibreel's dream of becoming the persecutor ends in insanity, as he is said to suffer from "paranoid schizophrenia" (*SV* 429).

As we have seen, the metamorphic bodies serve several functions in the context of the migrant's experience: while reflecting the racist attitude of the host society and Saladin's "problematic relationship to his own ethnic background" (Punday 813), they are also a means of literalising the migrants' "dream-like disorientation, their multiform, plural 'union-by-hybridization'" (Brennan 149).

5.4 Embodied Pluralism

Moraes Zogoiby, nicknamed 'Moor', is born ten years after Indian Independence. He is the embodiment of a new nation, but also that of India's colonial history that continues to exist in the form of a pluralist society. While *Midnight's Children* and *The Satanic Verses* are limited to India's colonial history with respect to the British Empire, *The Moor's Last Sigh* centres around earlier colonial connections (Portuguese, Spanish). The mode of embodiment in Rushdie's fifth major novel works on a different level than in his earlier ones. Moor is not so much the typical Indian, or 'type' of anything for that matter. His family tree is "unconventional", and so is Moraes himself; "his inescapable differentness is incompatible with the pinning down or pigeonholing of his life-story as representative of a particular category, class, race or period" (Gonzalez 103). Rather, Moor is an emblem "of India's apparent contradiction, a contradiction which contributes to its richness" (Gonzalez 102). With a Jewish father, a Christian mother, and Boabdil, the last Sultan of Granada, as well as Portuguese explorer Vasco da Gama as possible ancestors, Moor is representative of minorities as well as cultural diversity. He is, like Bombay, a product of "multiple ancestry" (Schülting 242). He is "both, and nothing: a jewholic-anonymous, a cathjew nut, a stewpot, a mongrel cur. [He] was -what's the word these days? - *atomised*. Yessir: a real Bombay mix. *Bastard* ... a smelly shit" (*MLS* 104). As the embodiment of minority, pluralism and hybridity, Moor mirrors Bombay, the "most cosmopolitan, most hybrid, most hotchpotch of Indian cities" (Rushdie, "In Good Faith" 404). Moraes calls himself a bastard, just like Bombay is "the bastard child of a Portuguese-English wedding" and yet "the most Indian of Indian cities" (*MLS* 350). Moor seems to defy all classification of collective identity - this impossibility of classification is what he paradoxically comes to embody: "I was a nobody from nowhere, like noone, belonging to nothing" (*MLS* 388).

Besides being an 'outcast' due to his cultural and ethnic roots, Moor's life is affected by physical peculiarities, a trait he shares with Saleem and Aadam. In *Midnight's Children*, 'Baby Saleem' grows like the post-independent Indian state, while Aadam hardly grows at all being born simultaneously with Emergency rule. Moor draws attention to the same aspect when telling us that he "grew in all directions" (*MLS* 188).[21] While descriptions of cities as bodies or body parts are common in Rushdie's writing, as Bombay is described as looking "like a hand but it's really a mouth, always open, always hungry, swallowing food and talent from everywhere else in India" (*MC* 172), the likening of Moor and his city is much stronger. Indeed, Moraes compares himself to "a skyscraper freed of all legal restraints, a one-man population explosion, a megalopolis, a shirt-ripping, button-popping Hulk" (*MLS* 188). He "represents the city itself" (Schultheis 580) as he "mushroom[s] into a huge urban sprawl of a fellow" (*MLS* 161).

---

[21] In *Midnight's Children*, the "accelerated history" of the time when Saleem is eleven is mentioned - this coincides not only with Saleem's growth, but also with the time of Moraes birth (*MC* 334), confirming the view that the protagonists' outstanding growth stands for a sense of acceleration in Indian history at that time.

However, Moor's main characteristic is not that he grows up to be taller than the Indian average, but that he grows fast: he suffers from a premature ageing disorder that lets him live life at twice the normal speed. After the birth of his elder sister, his mother Aurora Zogoiby wishes for a child "who gr[ows] up *really* fast" (*MLS* 141). When the Moor is born after only four and a half months of pregnancy, it seems like her 'wish' has come true. Instead of being born prematurely as one could have expected, Moor is born "post-mature[ly]" (*MLS* 144). On the one hand, this can be seen as a supernatural event typical of magic realist writing, an event which must be considered as having metaphorical implications. On the other hand, as Moor insists, there is "no need for supernatural explanations; some cock-up in the DNA will do" (*MLS* 145). This is a typical feature of Rushdie's writing; the reader is left in the dark about whether occurrences are to be explicated by a rational explanation or by magic. Irrespective of its cause, Moor's premature ageing can be read on several levels. Rushdie revealed in interviews that he sees it as a symptom of our time. Moor's disease stands for a specific mood that Rushdie aims to underline:

> I just thought that there is something in the air at the moment, that people think everything is speeding up, the pace of life, the rate of change, everything just seems to be going zooooom! And I thought that if there is a widespread sense of the acceleration of things, one way of crystallizing it was to make it happen to someone in a very literal way. (Rushdie, "The Salon Interview" 197)

However, the Moor's life 'on the fast lane' also works on a structural level. Rushdie wanted the book to have "a kind of acceleration, and urgency" (Rushdie, "All Things Considered" 189). The narrator's "personal calendar losing pages at superspeed" (*MLS* 152), his suffering from the disease of "being in a hurree", helps to achieve that sense of urgency (*MLS* 153). The reader stays aware throughout the novel that time is running out, especially since it is clear from the very first page of the novel that the narrator's time is drawing to a close. As Sabine Schülting pointed out, Moor's disease can also be seen as "an allusion to David Harvey's notion of space-time-compression in postmodernity" (251).[22] However, she interprets it as "a

[22] Harvey defines time-space-compression as "processes that so revolutionize the objective qualities of space and time that we are forced to alter, sometimes in quite radical ways, how we represent the world to ourselves" (Harvey 240).

metaphor for competing 'time-lines' in India – progressivism versus Hindu traditionalism" (251). It seems to be a valid reading, as this issue is presented through characters such as Moor's father Abraham, who as a businessman is a representative of progressivism, and Hindu fundamentalist Raman 'Mainduck' Fielding, who stands for traditionalism. What Schülting means in reference to Moor becomes clear when considering the following quotation:

> In Bombay, my old hovel'n'highrise home town, we think we're on top of the modern age, we boast that we're natural techno fast-trackers, but that's only true in the high-rises of our minds. Down in the slums of our bodies, we're still vulnerable to the most disorderly disorders, the scurviest of scurvies, the plaguiest of plagues. (*MLS* 145)

Moraes' disease expresses two ideologies that come to clash in Bombay. A problematic separation between body and mind becomes evident here: the mind is in a different time than the body; this incongruence can be seen as manifesting itself in Moor's body.[23] Referencing Bhabha's 'unhomeliness'[24], Schülting gives Moor's condition the fitting name of 'untimeliness' (cf. 251). His body is "the site of two incongruent time-systems ... Moraes's disease ... emphasizes the mere constructiveness of an individual biography, and, concurrently, of national history as linear 'life paths in time-space'" (251).

Moor's other characteristic is his "deformed right hand" that looks "like a club" (*MLS* 146). His deformed right hand is described as the hand of a boxer, "one to knock the whole world flat with" (*MLS* 147), "a hand to be reckoned with, a torpedo, a fist of fists" (*MLS* 195), a sleeping sword and a "fearsome fist" (*MLS* 241). As the Moor stands for a Muslim, Hindu, Catholic, Jewish *mélange*, I would like to read his deformed right hand as

---

23 The association of traditionalism with physicality, although restricted to a very male physicality, can also be seen in the description of the activities that the members of Mumbai's Axis take part in: "there would be arm-wrestling and mat-wrestling, push-up contests" until "the assembled company would arrive at a point of sweaty, brawling, raucous and finally exhausted nakedness" (*MLS* 300). "Now we are one", Fielding says after one of those events (*MLS* 300), which can be seen in the context of Joseph Alter's aforementioned assertion that training and rebuilding of bodies is associated with a rebuilding of the nation (17).

24 Bhabha calls 'unhomeliness' a "'paradigmatic colonial and postcolonial condition' that accompanies the psychic and geographical dislocations ... migration, diaspora, and exile" (Joseph 94; cf. Bhabha, *Location of Culture*).

standing for the potential of violence in this aggregation of cultural and religious difference. After all, only when using his hand for a fundamentalist cause does Moraes feel 'himself'.[25] Gonzales, in her analysis of Moor's deformity, combines two of the mentioned readings: "Moor has a symbolic function as an icon of the political mutilation of India and its accelerated historical development from colony to independent state to late twentieth-century high-tech society" (103). She sees his deformity and disorder as "the illustration of a confusing and sometimes tragic historical reality" (Gonzalez 103). When Aurora's art turns Moor's disfigurement, and thereby also that of the nation, into "a series of miracles" (*MLS* 224), "these depictions of the Moor's hand make vestiges of the colonial past into a new source of strength" (Schultheis 585).

Since Rushdie's use of palimpsest can be regarded as one of the most important stylistic and metaphorical devices in *The Moor's Last Sigh*, "a novel about layering" (Rushdie, "Bookworm" 204), his use of it shall be examined. The palimpsest motif is "criss-crossing with the idea of fragmentation" (Gonzalez 124), which has already been defined as an important aspect in the context of this paper. The most obvious examples are Vasco Miranda's painting of Aurora, which is covered with another painting, as well as the painting which reveals the identity of Aurora's murderer after the removal of its top layer. As "the city itself, maybe the whole country" is a palimpsest in Moor's story (*MLS* 184), Moor's identity might be seen as palimpsest in the widest sense: while in Bombay there is "Under World beneath Over World" (*MLS* 184), in Moraes, "a child's mind peered out ... through the portal's of a young man's beautiful body" (*MLS* 190). Mind and body form a palimpsest; they are layered but still discernible through one another, thereby changing the identity of the whole. Rather than serving to define an identity, however, "the palimpsest in *The Moor's Last Sigh* serve to thwart any endeavour to define identity once and for all" (Schülting 253).

Another stylistic method employed in *The Moor's Last Sigh* is that of ekphrasis. Moor's deformed hand is described as "misshapen as modern art itself" and as a "slip of the genius's brush" (*MLS* 147), thereby establishing the connection between his body and his mother's art. Moor has already been the subject of Aurora's art as a child: "charcoal sketches of me as a

25 The implications on his disability for his personal identity shall be scrutinized in Chapter 6.2.

young boy, sketches in which my ruined hand had been wondrously metamorphosed, becoming, variously, a flower, a paintbrush and a sword" (*MLS* 217). In her art, Aurora tries to give her son, "symbol ... of the new nation", a chance at being whole (*MLS* 303). The "fearsome fist" becomes a source of beauty and creativity in the paintings: "[i]n the 'early Moors' my hand was transformed into a series of miracles; often my body, too, was miraculously changed. In one picture - Courtship - I was Moor-as-peacock, spreading my many-eyed tail" (*MLS* 224). Pursuing the reading of Moor's hand as the expression of the fundamentalist threat or as an image of India's mutilation, Aurora's "palimpsest-art" seems to draw a utopian picture. She calls her utopia "Palimpstine", "[o]ne universe, one dimension, one country, one dream, bumpo'ing into one another, or being under, or on top of it" (*MLS* 226). Moraes, depicted as the Moor Sultan Boabdil, emerges in the centre of those fluid worlds. "This passage ... appears to be a straightforward and serious expression of history and identity, as forms of palimpsest. Palimpsests ... offer a suggestive model of hybrid identity", writes Huddart (107), although calling it a "straightforward" expression seems paradoxical when considering the amount of uncertainty that is innate in such an idea. Yet Moor himself is depicted as a palimpsest, as "a patchwork quilt of a man; or, as his old skin dropped from him chrysalis-fashion, standing revealed as a glorious butterfly" (*MLS* 227). In his depiction as the Moor, Moraes functions "not only as a representative of the nation and as a window into his own family's affairs but also ... as a symbol of the nation's long, complicated history" (Schultheis 585). As Gonzalez states,

> the heroine's art becomes increasingly representative of the embattled zone of India's identity, and history, just one of many 'petits récits' told from an openly subjective and minority point of view, instead of constituting an imposed epic or "grand narrative" to which the reader is subjected. (126)

Once again, the private becomes public, and Moor's body is at the centre of the 'embattled zone'. Moor, however, who acts as "a unifier of opposites, a standard bearer of pluralism" in her earlier paintings, loses that "metaphorical role", "ceasing to stand as a symbol - however approximate - of the new nation, and being transformed, instead, into a semi-allegorical figure of decay" (*MLS* 303). Aurora's paintings offer a view of modern Indian society and therefore must also "document the decline of India's idealistic pluralism" (Schultheis 577). While, as Moor promised, "ruined limbs play a central role in our saga", detached limbs feature in Aurora's art as well (*MLS* 139). The first time Moor mentions their central role, however, they are connected to colonialism:

> The first point to note is that people's limbs got detached more easily in those days. The banners of British domination hung over the country like strips of flypaper, and, in trying to unstick ourselves from those fatal flags, we flies - if I may use the term 'we' to refer to a time before my birth - would often leave legs or wings behind, preferring freedom to wholeness. Of course now, that the sticky paper is ancient history, we find ways of losing our limbs in the struggle against other equally lethal, equally acquainted, equally adhesive standard of our own devising. (*MLS* 129)

In the context of colonialism, the image of detached limbs or 'amputation' reminds the reader familiar with Frantz Fanon of his usage of the image of amputation. He likens the colonial experience of being disempowered to form one's own identity to an 'amputation' (cf. *Black Skin, White Masks*). "The violence of this 'revision' of ... identity is conveyed powerfully in the image of amputation" (McLeod, *Beginning Postcolonialism* 20). As Berlant puts it in his book *The Anatomy of National Fantasy*, "the colonized subject becomes a part-object, or, 'amputation,' to himself, without a nation to be 'sheltered behind.' National identity provides, then, a translation of the historical subject into an 'Imaginary' realm of ideality and wholeness" (qtd. in Kortenaar 72). Unsticking themselves from the flypaper of imperial power, the colonised peoples gain freedom, but remain partial and incomplete. In a postcolonial society, it is difficult for the "fractured and alienated third-world subject" to identify with their 'new nation' and achieve wholeness in that sense (Uprety 379). The theme of partiality brings us back to Aurora's art and postcolonial society. Her collage-art conveys the image of amputation, as it likens the situation of national upheaval to the experience of amputation. In her later pieces

> it was the people themselves who were made of rubbish, who were collages composed of what the metropolis did not value: lost buttons, broken windscreen wipers, torn cloth, burned books, exposed camera film. They even went scavenging for their own limbs: discovering great heaps of severed body parts, they pounced on what they lacked, and they weren't too particular, couldn't afford to be choosers, so that many of them ended up with two left

> feet or gave up the search for buttocks and fixed a pair of plump amputated breasts where their missing behinds should be. (*MLS* 302)

Both references to detached body parts reveal (post)colonial society's problematic relationship to national identity. While Aurora's previous work celebrated motifs of hybridity and pluralism, the same ideas are turned into images of waste and monstrosity; their "potential for darkness" is illustrated in her art (*MLS* 303). The human collages in Aurora's work foreshadow the downfall of Bombay due to Muslim-Hindu violence, when beyond Aurora's canvas "bits of bodies [are] lying everywhere; human and animal blood, guts and bones" (*MLS* 372). The human body becomes a bomb as Moor writes that the explosions that destroy the city "burst out of [their] very own bodies. [They] were both the bombers and the bombs" (*MLS* 372). Again we can detect a parallel between Moor's body and Bombay: "The city I knew was dying. The body I inhabited, ditto" (*MLS* 374). The city that Moraes leaves towards the end of the story is no longer Moor's Bombay, "no longer the city of mixed-up mongrel joy" (*MLS* 376).

6. Questions of Personal Identity

When narrators and protagonists in Rushdie's novels ask themselves "Who am I?" (*SV* 4; 191), "Who what am I? (*MC* 535), or conclude in Cartesian terms: "*Suspiro ergo sum.* I sigh therefore I am" (*MLS* 53), the theme of personal identity is revealed as pervasive. Anita Desai remarked in a review that "while individual history does not make sense unless seen against its national background, neither does national history make sense unless seen in the form of individual lives and histories" (qtd. in Smale 64). Having considered individual histories and the protagonists' bodies as symptoms of their (trans)national backgrounds on an allegorical level, their individual lives and histories shall be considered, and their identities shall be analysed, on a private level. The characters shall not be regarded as standing for a certain type, but simply as individuals standing for themselves in contemporary society. However, it is important to keep Desai's assumption in mind insofar as the protagonists' (trans)national backgrounds should not and cannot be factored out completely.

6.1 Genealogy

> In conservative romance the truth of identity is a question of parentage. Discover who your parents or ancestors were, and you also discover who you are and where you should be. Identity is inherited and able to be bequeathed to future generations because ultimately it is located in the genes or, as romance is more likely to put it, in the blood. Blood established identity in the form of nobility, race, or a legal claim to property status. (Kortenaar 196)[26]

This quotation draws attention to the importance of genealogy to a person's identity, whether to social or personal self-understanding. As a discussion of the genre of romance is out of place here, the quotation should be seen as merely serving as a starting point to scrutinize the treatment of genealogy in the novels under discussion. It is obvious, however, that we must find its position challenged.

---

26 This quotation stems from Kortenaar's discussion of contrasting understandings of geneology and identity in realism and conservative romance (see 193–198). He regards Saleem's story a "parody of romance", while Shiva's story is seen by him as a "muted form of a conservative romance" (197).

As Foucault points out in "Nietzsche, Genealogy, History", where history is opposed to the search for genealogy, "descent attaches itself to the body" (82). The concept of genealogy connects the aspect identity and the body. That the idea of genealogy is significant in *Midnight's Children* as well as in *The Moor's Last Sigh* can be seen from the fact that both novels start, in a Shandeanly manner, decades before the respective narrators' births. As the body can be read as the external expression of origins, it will prove interesting to consider the protagonists' physiques in the context of their ancestry. Saleem starts his narration with the story of his grandfather Aadam Aziz, the description of whose nose, "a cyranose", "a proboscissimus" is especially significant (*MC* 9). Indeed, two of Saleem's main physical features are his nose and his blue eyes - both are attributed to his grandfather. His nose is seen as a proof of his origins: "I wish to place on record my gratitude to this mighty organ - if not for it, who would ever have believed me to be truly my mother's son, my grandfather's grandson? - this colossal apparatus which was to be my birthright, too" (*MC* 9). In fact, as the reader learns at a later point, his biological mother Vanita, the wife of a poor Hindu street singer, has had an affair with the Englishman Methwold and Saleem is swapped with 'real' midnight's child Shiva in the hospital crib. Saleem's blue eyes are not inherited from his Kashmiri grandfather but from his English father, while his characteristic nose is to be attributed to his French ancestors. As the family Saleem speaks about in the first fourth of his story turns out to be not his (biological) family, attention is drawn to the illusory and fictional nature of origins as well as to the ambiguous nature of parentage. By the time he writes down his story, Saleem knows of the baby switch. Nevertheless, he begins his own story with that of Aadam Aziz, thus making a statement about the fictional nature inherent to personal history, which is "always an invention and is not more fictional because it lacks a biological base. Blood ties are metaphor" in *Midnight's Children* (Kortenaar 36).

Rushdie's playful treatment of the idea of deceptive origins is carried to extremes in an episode in which the Aziz's family dogs are described. When the family's mongrel dog dies of a burst artery, Ahmed Sinai gets Saleem an Alsatian puppy, a pedigree dog. This dog, named Baroness Simki von der Heiden, however, dies of syphilis, a disease clearly connected to promiscuity, therefore ridiculing its false pedigree (cf. *MC* 283).

By mocking Ahmed Sinai's belief in the noble origins of the dog, Rushdie once again draws attention to the fact that origins can be illusory, maybe fictional. Ahmed himself invents ancestors to impress Methwold and soon afterwards fails to distinguish between his lie and reality (cf. *MC* 282).

Another layer of absurdity and irony is added when the genealogical line is re-established: Saleem's adoptive son Aadam, whose biological father is Shiva, is restored to his 'true' genealogical line; Saleem is not Aadam's grandson, but Aadam is his great-grandfather's 'real' great-grandson. Although the reader has learned before that those physical 'proofs' are illusory, another supposed confirmation for that relation is offered in Aadam's eyes, coloured "the fateful blue of Kashmiri sky" (*MC* 594), and his gigantic ears, as "elephantiasis attacked him in the ears instead of the nose ... he was elephant-headed Ganesh" (*MC* 587), just like his biological grandfather (*MC* 9). On an allegorical level, those genealogical connections "starkly [dramatize] the illusion of coherence upon which postcolonial nationality rests" and also importantly, ideas of blood and race as the unifying constituents of national identity are unmasked (Kane 96). One should not forget, however, that these complications also dramatize the illusion of coherence upon which a traditional sense of self-identity rests on the individual level.

The theme of disputed parentage plays an important role in *Midnight's Children*. That is why Ganesh, the deity frequently referred to in the novel, is seen by Rushdie as "a proper mythological character to place behind Saleem": apart from a big nose they share the burden of a disputed parentage (Rushdie, "*Midnight's Children*" 8–9).[27] Saleem himself, "fathered by history", claims multiple parents. This fact can be read as another expression of Saleem's search for identity and underlines his fragmentation. Among others, "Picture Singh is one of Saleem's 'fathers,' along with Aadam Sinai (whose wife brings the Kashmiri inheritance), William Methwold (representing the colonial debt), and General Zulfikar (standing for Islamic military tradition), each of whom represents a part of the India which is summoned up by Saleem" (Brigg 180). Saleem chooses his parents; they are not "organically imposed" (Kane 96). The importance of origins to

27 The other important connection between Ganesh and Saleem is that of writing. By comparing himself to Ganesh, Saleem underlines his identity as a writer as Ganesh is said to have written down the *Mahabharata* and is the god of memory.

a person's identity and sense of belonging becomes apparent in the chapter that Saleem entitles "Alpha and Omega", in which he and his parents are unexpectedly confronted with the mystery of Saleem's genealogy.

Origins, both ancient and modern, are also doubtful in *The Moor's Last Sigh*. By informing the reader of his mother's meeting "with the Prime Minister of India, nine months before [he] was born" (*MLS* 175), Moraes opens up the possibility of his being conceived during his mother's affair with Nehru, which would make his double-quick gestation a myth. Moreover, his older ancestry, his connection to Boabdil the Moor, is treated in an ambiguous manner. If descent "inscribes itself in the nervous system, in temperament, in the digestive apparatus; it appears in faulty respiration, in improper diets, in the debilitated and prostrate bodies of those whose ancestors committed errors" (Foucault 82), Moor's asthma must be considered as an indicator and a symptom of his origins. In the account of his parents' lives before his own birth, Moraes describes his father's asthma as meaningful:

> Breath left his body with a whine, and the next breath was a gasp. The onset of asthma (more asthma! It's a wonder I can breathe at all!) was like an omen, a joining of lives across the centuries, or so Abraham fancied as he grew into his manhood and the illness gained in strength. These wheezing sighs not only mine, but his. The eyes hot with ancient grief. Boabdil, I too am thy mother's son. (*MLS* 80)

Here, the genealogical connection is drawn by means of a physical defect. Similarly, Moor's exclamation that his "perspiration had acquired a peppery smell" (*MLS* 245), must also be read as a reference to his parents, who had made "pepper love" when they first fell in love and are said to be connected forever through their "pepper'n'spice sweat" (*MLS* 90). Almost ironically, Moor talks about his sister's death as if it was another confirmation of the family's genealogy: "My sister perished of – what else? – a shortage of breath... . She died in pop-eyed agony, retching and gasping for air, while poison ate her lungs" (*MLS* 275–276). In spite of the meaningful ambiguity associated with origins, the asthma serves to connect different times. It makes an identification of Moraes with Boabdil possible and connects different layers of genealogy, giving them a sense of continuity. At the same time, it is also suggested that the material proof of a genealogical connection to Boabdil, a crown, was not inherited but simply stolen: "never mind about genetics; just follow the cash" (*MLS* 85).

For Saladin Chamcha, the aspect of origins is an ambiguous topic. He tries to counteract the assumption that origins or genealogy are connected with the formation of identity. Ironically, a part of him still seems to believe that his DNA is the only thing that prevents him from being completely English. His genetic inheritance, "his own chromosomes, two sticks too long, or too short, he couldn't remember", forbids him to have children (*SV* 50). For Saladin, not being able to procreate, not being able to have children with his *English* wife, seems to be a setback in the complete conquest of Englishness. He feels betrayed by his inheritance; after all, "were genetics his responsibility?" (*SV* 257).

In *Midnight's Children* and *The Satanic Verses*, the protagonists are confronted with the question of how identity is formed; Saleem as a result of the 'baby switch' and Saladin as a consequence of migration. Both are shown as defying the "romantic" notion that identity is given and based on blood ties instead of being a product of social interaction and construction. However, a straightforward view is not suggested by Rushdie, as shall be outlined in the course of this chapter.

6.2 (W)holes and Fragments

Ute Manecke writes in her dissertation that "Anglo-Indian novels tackle the theme of wholeness particularly in respect to the Independence struggle in the country", thus connecting it to national identity, and that "later novels increasingly focus on the formation of hybridities that evolve in the context of migration" (Manecke 99). The way in which wholeness and fragmentation are significant in the context of India's and Britain's national background has been presented in the former chapter. In the characters' more personal life, the aspect of wholeness is worth considering in respect of the body as well. The term 'wholeness' can be related to a physical as well as a psychological state. It is defined on the one hand as "soundness, freedom from injury" but also as "the character of having nothing wanting, or of having all its parts in due connexion", "completeness, perfection" ("Wholeness"). That the term must be a problematic one in the contemporary identity discourse should be clear when looking back at the concept of personal identity: if being whole means being "undivided", it will prove interesting to scrutinize the protagonists' ability to achieve that "quality of constituting a complex unity" ("Wholeness").

6.2.1 *Images of Wholeness*

In *Midnight's Children*, the theme of wholeness is introduced by means of a very physical image. In the beginning of the novel, Aadam Aziz returns from Germany where he received medical training. Back in Kashmir, he realises that his worldview has changed and that this change entails the loss of religious certainty. Consequently, his body becomes the subject of a "permanent alteration": in the centre of his body appears a "hole ... the size of a melon" (*MC* 7; *MC* 21). His spiritual doubts, epitomized in his physical alteration, underline Aadam's role as the embodiment of the 'modern man'. Belief is big part of tradition, and the lack of certainty of faith seems to be one expression of his attitude. The hole becomes the physical marker of his loss of faith and manifests the feeling of incompleteness that goes along with it. It feels like a "hole at the heart of his very self" (Booker 994), while the fact that the hole in his body reappears shortly before his death shows how it turns "him into just another shrivelled, empty old man, over whom the God (and other superstitions) against which he'd fought for so long was beginning to reassert His dominion" (*MC* 260). Here, the hole serves to emphasise the fact that despite Aadam's consistent convictions, a part of him remains inchoate. "To have a self is paradoxically to be missing something", writes Kortenaar in his analysis of *Midnight's Children* (100), pointing out that by reasserting his personal convictions and thereby his individuality, Aadam may come to lack something else. Interestingly, Saleem inherits the hole standing for the "failure to believe or disbelieve in God", but from his grandfather (*MC* 382). Furthermore, the hole can be read as a representation of the fact that he, like Aadam Aziz, "owes his identity to an 'inbetween' space of hybridity and exchange" (Uprety 373). The hole Saleem feels in himself is "occupied ... by [his] voices" for a long time – Saleem manages to fill this void with another physical entity: the other children of midnight (*MC* 266). He is literally made whole again by encompassing the multitude of the children of midnight, though only temporarily.

The idea of wholeness is taken very literally and inverted in the characters' physical 'incompleteness', as parts of their bodies are missing.

Saleem's disintegration as well as his grandfather's, which anticipates Saleem's fate, is to be read along these lines. In *Midnight's Children*, bodies are shown as incomplete or fragmented when identities become unstable, just as identities can become unstable as a consequence of lack of bodily wholeness. This 'technique' seems to work both ways. When Saleem lives with Parvati the Witch, the marks of mutilation and imperfection on his body begin to vanish: he starts to grow hair where he thought hair would never grow again, and birthmarks fade away (*MC* 561). However, the effects of the ectomy that is a "sperectomy" make Saleem's physical afflictions return (*MC* 624). This shows how faith, as well as hope or optimism, is treated as a physical entity that can leave a hole or an absence behind. Saleem's lack of wholeness is also mirrored in the image he sees of his sister Jamila, who has "begun to rot" (*MC* 553). "The rotting body, no less than the idealized body, reflects something within the observer, a fundamental incompleteness" (Kortenaar 103), which points to Saleem's longing for national wholeness, that Jamila has come to represent.[28]

Gibreel Farishta's loss of faith is strongly connected to the physical experience of a nearly fatal disease. In this case the uncertainty of his religious identity is not the cause of physical alteration; on the contrary it is his physical unsoundness that triggers the identity crisis. That he is going through a very personal and existential experience is hinted at in the nature of his disease: he haemorrhages on his insides, "bleeding to death inside his skin", while his outer body seems to remain undamaged (*SV* 28). The fact that the bleeding continues for seven days while doctors are unable to effectively treat the mysterious disease, highlights the idea that it represents more than a bodily malfunction. In fact, the time of his illness turns out to be a metamorphic experience. Gibreel comes to doubt the existence of God (Allah) and finally to accept the emptiness that he feels: "On that day of metamorphosis the illness changed and the recovery began" (*SV* 30). When

28 However, the more obvious reading is that Jamila's rotting image reflects Saleem's guilt over falling in love with his sister (although he does so only after it turns out he is not her biological brother): "the dreadful pustules and cankers of forbidden love were spreading across her face ... , the rancid flowers of incest blossomed on my sister's phantasmal features" (*MC* 553). Just as Joseph Da Costa's decomposition (*MC* 350), Musa's (Ahmed's servant who had stolen from the household), leprosy (*MC* 390) and Rekha Merchant's ghost in *The Satanic Verses* are manifestations of guilt.

Gibreel leaves India to find Alleluia Cone, the woman he falls in love with after his recovery, "the ubiquitous images of his face [begin] to rot" (*SV* 15):

> Cardboard effigies of Gibreel were seen to decay and list. Dangling limply on their sustaining scaffolds, they lost arms, withered, snapped at the neck ... At last his images simply faded off the printed page, so that the shiny covers ... went blank at the bookstalls and their publishers fired the printers and blamed the quality of the ink. Even on the silver screen itself ... that supposedly immortal physiognomy began to putrefy, blister and bleach. (*SV* 16)

This reflects the film star's journey "out of the screen into the world" (*SV* 13), his "vanishing ... *into thin air*" (*SV* 11). As he 'migrates' to London, he sees himself as his own reincarnation, as he has died twice 'almost', "so it adds up, it counts" (*SV* 31). He is "a new man with a new life" (*SV* 31). The 'old' Gibreel of the images on the film posters, his body that had been India's avatar, fades and crumbles away.

6.2.2 Personal Identity and the Body

While bodily defects and imperfections have been described as reflecting a character's identity crisis or lack of wholeness in a metaphorical (although literalised) manner, an additional aspect shall be taken into account: the fact that a person's bodily characteristics can have a considerable effect on a person's personal identity. Saleem as well as Moor suffer from their physical peculiarities, from their 'grotesque' bodies. Saleem cannot stand the way he looks; his self-abhorrence comes to change the way others perceive him. This happens quite literally in the Midnight's Children Conference: "my picture of myself was heavily distorted by my own self-consciousness about my appearance; so that the portrait I sent across the thought-waves of the nation ... was about as hideous a portrait as could be" (*MC* 304). Saleem is given nicknames like "Snotnose, Sniffer, Mapface" by his classmates, reducing him to his grotesqueness and making him feel isolated, even monstrous (*MC* 534). Moor feels similarly 'different' due to his handicap that makes "young ladies shudder fastidiously, reminding them of life's ugliness" (*MLS* 241). He feels like a "freak" (cf. *MLS* 240); even his mother thinks that "nothing that grew-o'ed so fast could have grown right" and seems to find her son's deformity repulsive (*MLS* 146). For a long time Saleem accepts and even seems to understand "how parents and strangers ... legitimately despise or exile him for his ugliness" (*MC*

534). The protagonists grotesqueness and monstrosity that demonstrate societal ills in *The Satanic Verses*, come to serve an additional purpose: to illustrate the protagonists' inner struggles connected to their quest for wholeness.

As Saleem puts the problem of identity in terms of an opposition of the inside and the outside that will be regarded in the next subchapter, Moor exemplifies the problems connected specifically to the oppositions of body and self. As his right hand is deformed he is forced to live his life as a left-handed person. This is problematic for him as he is not 'naturally' left-handed: "it turned out I was a right-handed entity, a dexter whose right hand just happened to be a wreck" (*MLS* 153). His deformity prevents him from being 'himself'. Referring to his ageing disorder, Moraes asserts that his "inside and outside have always been out of sync" (*MLS* 162). As a young boy he has a sexual relationship with his home schooling teacher Dilly Hormuz. Here, the opposition between his two selves, his 'bodily self' and his 'mental/spiritual self' is contrasted: when Dilly caresses him, his 'internal self' accepts her caresses as the "innocent gestures of the love" he desperately needs, while his body is "capable of wholly adult responses" (*MLS* 190). His ageing disorder makes him feel

> like a visitor from another dimension, another time-line... Four and a half months from conception to birth ... the swelling of [his mother's] womb, it resembles nothing so much as a movie special effect, as if under the influence of some twice-pushed genetic button her biochemical pixels had gone loco and begun to morph her protesting body so violently that the speeded-up outward effects of my gestation actually became visible to the naked eye. (*MLS* 144)

In this passage it becomes very obvious that Moor feels like an "alien" (*MLS* 241), someone who does not belong where he is. His teacher Dilly is the first person to make him feel whole, since she accepts him without considering the discrepancy between his body-self and inner-self. However, Moor comes to feel like time is moving at his own double speed, and he no longer perceives himself as "a young man trapped inside an old – or rather, to borrow the lingo of the city's textile industry, 'antiqued', even 'distressed' – covering of skin" (*MLS* 241). Instead, he feels his "outer apparent age" becomes his age (*MLS* 241). He adapts his identity to what his appearance dictates. However, when his lover Uma sees "a young guy" in him "looking out at [her]", he realises that this is his "true self" (*MLS* 245). As we can see, Moor goes through a development, or rather, through constant re-negotiations, trying to unite his conflicting identities. His insecurities and longing for direction become apparent when considering the way he chooses to deal with his other handicap.

Moraes life changes when he is exiled by his parents. The extreme effect his mother's repudiation has on him is potently depicted in the image of flaying, which is introduced in the character of Carmen da Gama, who dreams of being flayed as "an expression of sexual guilt that longs for ablation" (Grant 113). In Carmen's dream ("flay me flay my skin from my body whole entire and let me start again let me be of no race no name no sex" [*MLS* 47]), skin becomes an image of "the existential marking between the self and the world" (Taylor 105). Furthermore, in the character of Oliver D'Aeth it is seen in its function as the representation of social identity: "We will never gain humanity until we loose our skins" (*MLS* 95). When Moor dreams of "peeling off [his] skin plaintain-fashion, of going forth naked into the world, like an anatomy illustration from *Encyclopaedia Britannica* ... set free from the otherwise inescapable jails of colour, race and clan" (*MLS* 136), skin is once again represented as a layer of "social self and emotional paint, rituals and rules" (Taylor 105). The shedding of one's skin is associated with "going beyond the self that we may discover our true human value" and is invested with a positive meaning in these examples (Grant 113). Moor longs for being human, without being subject to classification. However, to get back to the initial point, when Moor is repudiated by his mother and in Bombay's underworld in prison, the image takes on terrifying form:

> I felt that my skin was indeed coming away from my body, as I had dreamed so long ago that it would. But in this version of the dream, my peeling skin took with it all elements of my personality. I was becoming nobody, nothing; or rather, I was becoming what had been made of me... . I was scum. (*MLS* 288)

This quotation is to be read in the contexts of Moor's loss of family. The exile imposed on him by his mother is "the real psychological violence that translates into such physical terms" (Grant 114). Moraes imagines how his mother would "squash" out the air of his being, which is a "shape without frontiers, a self without walls" (*MLS* 288).

On his 'quest for wholeness', Moraes, who considers his deformed hand his fate (cf. *MLS* 240), embraces his destiny and joins the Hindu fundamentalist party Mumbai's Axis. As a member of the MA, Moor comes to make brutal use of his deformed hand, which gifted him with a talent for boxing, as he works as a professional thug. This can be read as an implementation of a 'Trotzidentität', an identity of defiance. Similar to the immigrant community embracing the image of the devil in *The Satanic Verses*, Moor resolves to clasp the names given to him - "outcast, outlaw, untouchable, disgusting, vile" to his bosom and "make [his] own", mainly in reaction to the exile imposed on him by his parents (*MLS* 296).

Moor's joining of the MA can be seen as an example of the following statement:

> Those stigmatized within a community because of a physical disability ... may critically reflect on their 'spoiled identity', discover that they are much more capable than society assumes, and reject their bodily identity in favour of a radical alternative. (Shilling 201)

When Moor resolves to join Mumbai's Axis, it is in order to fully *become* his fate, to be "a Hammer, not a Moor" (*MLS* 295). His deformed hand, formerly hidden and considered shameful, is now displayed openly and with pride. It becomes the source of Moor's "true self" (*MLS* 295): "I need no longer be what ancestry, breeding and misfortune had decreed, but could enter, at long last, into myself... . Henceforth I would be my fist" (*MLS* 295).

In a certain way, his joining the Mumbai's Axis for a fundamentalist cause can be read as reminiscent of Shakespeare's *Richard III*, in which the Duke of Gloucester, who suffers from physical deformities, states: "And therefore, since I cannot prove a lover ... I am determined to prove a villain" (Shakespeare 1.1.28-30). By drawing attention to the question whether "discernible defects reveal the presence of an equally defective moral and civil character" (Mitchell 13), the connection between body and destiny - a seemingly unalterable predetermined identity that is relevant also for an analysis of Moraes - is established. The idea that physical features determine or restrict a person's individuality is a striking aspect in a discussion of personal identity and the body in Rushdie's fiction. For Moor, 'becoming' his fist seems to be a way to achieve a long lacked harmony of body and self.

In *Midnight's Children* this idea is addressed as well. Saleem describes his cousin Zafar Zulfikar as being "doomed" by his incontinence (*MC* 464), while in *The Satanic Verses*, Allie Cone, a mountaineer "betrayed by [her] feet", is not able to live out her personal dreams due to physical restrictions caused by her fallen arches (*SV* 197). Moor depicts his outstanding growth and size as "succeed[ing] in tying [him] down" (*MLS* 188). As he is rejected by schools due to his deceivingly mature appearance, he is home schooled and becomes socially isolated. He connects both issues by stating that "the wider [his] physical bounds were set, the more limited [his] horizons seemed to become" (*MLS* 188).

The body is shown as a main factor in identity construction. The self has to position itself in relation to the body for a person to be able to achieve a harmonious identity. Discrepancies between what one believes oneself to be and what other people see, as well as bodily restraints have to be taken into account in order to become one's 'true self'. One has to 'make sense' of one's body and incorporate it in one's self-understanding.

6.2.3 Continuity

While the question of continuity has been central to the discourse on identity in its beginnings, it remains a very important point of discussion especially in contemporary discourse. As Rushdie's novels are commonly seen as dealing with certain aspects in an entirely postmodern way, the treatment of personal identity shall be discussed in those terms. While this approach as well as the perspective of postcolonial theory indicate a rather Western approach, Rushdie's writing, famous for its incorporation of both Eastern and Western traditions, is revealed as hybrid. A predominantly Indian concept that broaches the issue of continuous identities is that of reincarnation. In the character of Joseph Da Costa in *Midnight's Children*, Rushdie approaches this concept in a satirical manner: even after his death, Joseph "is there each night, sometimes in human form, but not always, sometimes he's a wolf, or a snail, once a broomstick" (*MC* 237). The idea of reincarnation is also taken up in *The Satanic Verses*, first and foremost in the protagonist's fall from the sky and the opening words of the novel: "To be born again ... first you have to die" (*SV* 3). Furthermore, Saladin suggests that Gibreel's dreams are a sign of his undergoing a metamorphosis: "maybe that's what's happening to you, loudmouth, your old self is dying and that dream-angel of yours is trying to be born into your flesh" (*SV* 85). Thereby, the concept of reincarnation not only introduces the question of what happens to the soul when the body dies, but also the idea of multiple or exchangeable selves respectively inhabiting one body. The concept reiterates the link between body and identity, a connection that shall be taken into account in the following discussion as well. This most illustrative example will prove to be, once again, that of metamorphosis.

Postmodern notions of identity are discussed in *The Satanic Verses*, whereat the temporality of identity is explicitly dealt with. Saladin is the main representative of characters displaying the 'postmodern condition' and a prime example of identity transformation. When he was younger, he experimented with multiple identities: "Each self he tried on, had seemed reassuringly temporary. Its imperfections didn't matter because he could easily replace one moment by the next, one Saladin by another" (*SV* 63). After moving to Britain as a young boy, Chamcha makes the "conquest of Englishness" his obsession (*SV* 257). He, who has always wanted to live in Britain, decides to reject his Indian identity once and for all and 'work' on a new British identity. His creation of a new identity goes along with the construction of a new face which he comes to think of "as *his own*" (*SV* 33). Moreover, he "shape[s] himself a voice to go with the face" (*SV* 33). Very consciously, Chamcha forms his new self by means of suppressing his roots and changing his outward appearance, as if one was not possible without the other. But, as Chamcha has to find out, "when one radically shifts identity at will, one might lose control" (Kellner qtd. in Baumann 18). During and after his first return to Bombay in fifteen years, where he plays the role of an Indian in a play, he realises that his 'old' self is coming back to him. Having thought of his Indian self as dead, he must become conscious that it is everything but "a dead self, a shadow" (*SV* 58). He is confronted with his 'old self', which threatens to destabilize his assiduously constructed identity. His realisation of that fact is connected to his physical changes. He finds "his voice betraying himself" by falling back into the Indian way of speaking that he has to bring back to life for his part in the play (*SV* 49). Later, as he begins an affair with Zeeny Vakil, the woman determined to bring back 'the Indian' in him, "he discover[s] his component parts to be capable of other treasons too" (*SV* 49). By calling it treason, he implies that his body acts against his (British) self and in line with his well-suppressed

Indian self. The aspect of the body displaying 'a life of its own' shall be given further attention at a later point. Saladin tries to play down his attraction to Zeeny as mere physical appeal. Back in England, at a later point, when he finds himself thinking of Hyacinth, his nurse in the detention centre, he considers his "romantic notions about a black woman" a proof of his continuing metamorphosis (*SV* 170).

On the plane back to England, he dreams of "a bizarre stranger, a man with glass skin, who rapped his knuckles mournfully against the thin, brittle membrane covering his entire body and begged Saladin to help him, to release him from the prison of his skin" (*SV* 34). Waking up from this dream, he speaks with a strange Bombay accent. According to Steven Walker,

> the most obvious interpretation of this dream is cultural and political: imprisoned as though by glass skin in his postcolonial anglophilia, Saladin needs to regain contact with native culture, to free his Indian self from the proper English persona in which he has enclosed himself, English accent and all. (362)

When Gibreel and Saladin awake on an English beach after their fall, Saladin's body is "cased in a fine skin of ice, smooth as glass, like a bad dream come true" (*SV* 131) – "the man with the glass skin is him" (Walker 363).

The mutation of "Salahuddin Chamchawala into Saladin Chamcha" has not only been a transformation of identity, but has generated physical changes as well (*SV* 37). The instability of identity is highlighted once again by means of physical symptoms: in India, not only Chamcha's voice changes but he also feels "irregular palpitations" in his chest (*SV* 57). Those symptoms lead him to compare India to a disease which he had thought himself immune to:

> After you recover from typhoid, Chamcha reflected, you remain immune to the disease for ten years or so. But nothing is forever; eventually the antibodies vanish from your blood. He had to accept the fact that his blood no longer contained the immunizing agents that would have enabled him to suffer India's reality. (*SV* 57)

Chamcha's only problem seems to be of a physical nature. The antibodies that kept his Indian self, the Indian 'disease' out of his body are receding.

While we have considered the consequences of his crossing of the boundaries on his social and ethnic identity, the consequences on his sense of self-identity are illustrated here. Confronted with the personal implications of migration, they become physical symptoms visible on the body. With regard to personal identity, migration must be seen as more than the literal act of crossing physical boundaries. As mentioned above, for Rushdie, migration itself is a kind of metamorphosis and the consequences of migration are "one of the classic contemporary locations of metamorphosis" (Rushdie, "Between God and Devil" 95). There is a firm link between metamorphosis and "the act of traveling" (Rushdie, "Between God and Devil" 95). Rushdie himself explained in an interview that his fourth novel is

> a novel in which people change shape, and which addresses the great questions about a change of shape ... which were posed by Ovid: about whether a change in form was a change in kind. Whether there is an essence in us which survives transmutation, given that, even if we don't change into cloven-hoofed creatures, there is a great deal of change in everybody's life. The question is whether or not there is an essential centre... . The [novel] uses the idea of metamorphoses to discuss that. (Rushdie, "Salman Rushdie Talks" 218)

One of the most important intertexts for the discussion of the aspect of personal identity has thereby been named by Rushdie himself: Ovid's *Metamorphoses*. It is introduced in the very beginning of the novel when we are told how Gibreel devoured "the metamorphic myths of Greece and Rome, the avatars of Jupiter, the boy who became a flower, the spiderwoman" (*SV* 23-24), while it later becomes the starting point of Sufyan's analysis of Chamcha's transformation:

> Question of mutability of the essence of the self ... has long been subject of profound debate. For example, great Lucretius tells us, in *De Rerum Natura*, this following thing: ... 'Whatever by its changing goes out of its frontiers' ... 'by doing so brings immediate death to its old self'. However ... poet Ovid, in the *Metamorphoses*, takes diametrically opposed view. He avers thus: 'As yielding wax' – heated, you see, possibly for the sealing of documents or such, - 'is stamped with new designs And changes shape and seems not still the same, Yet is indeed the same, even to our souls,' – you hear, good sir? Our spirits! Our immortal essences! – 'Are still the same forever, but adopt In their migrations ever-varying forms.' (*SV* 276-277)

Chamcha must choose to either "accept Lucretius and conclude that some demonic and irreversible mutation is taking place in [his] inmost depths, or

... go with Ovid and concede that everything now emerging is no more than a manifestation of what was already there" (*SV* 277). Unlike his landlord Sufyan, he cannot seem to believe in his immortal essence and chooses

> Lucretius over Ovid. The inconstant soul the mutability of everything, das Ich, every last speck. A being going through life can become so other to himself as to be another, discrete, severed from history ... He would enter into his new self; he would be what he had become: loud, stenchy, hideous, outsize, grotesque, inhuman, powerful. (*SV* 288-289)

After his transformation into an Englishman has backfired, Saladin decides to see himself as someone altogether new. Not believing in his own immutable essence, he decides to be what his body dictates him to be and embraces discontinuity. As mentioned above, changing himself used to be easy for him, just like in his job as a voice artist, where he and his partner Mimi "changed their voices along with their clothes, ... or their features and limbs, because they were capable of changing all of them, switching legs, arms, noses, ears, eyes" (*SV* 62). In a world constructed of disposable products, "identities can be adopted and discarded like a change of costume" (Lasch qtd. in Baumann 23). Now, however, as change begins "to feel painful; the arteries of the possible" have begun to harden, Saladin seems to have come to a crossroad in his life (*SV* 63).

While on the social level, Chamcha's metamorphosis becomes part of an anti-racist discourse, on the more personal level, it stands for "the repressed side of his prim and toadyish personality" (Walker 359). Walker, who analyses Saladin and Gibreel's identity crises by means of a Jungian approach, sees Saladin's goatish physique as an "embodiment of his repressed vitality, social rebellion, hatred, and rage" (Walker 359). His old self comes to haunt him as a shadow (cf. *SV* 58) until he himself turns into that very shadow. The narrator warns Saladin to "[w]atch out, Chamcha, look out for your shadow. That black fellow creeping up behind", in vain (*SV* 53). This interpretation is confirmed in the description of the circumstances in which Saladin regains his human form: when the monster that is Saladin "fixes its mind upon its foe ... it felt within itself the most inexplicable sensations of compression, suction, withdrawal; it was racked by terrible, squeezing pains" (*SV* 294). When 'the monster' wakes up the next morning it has become "Mr Saladin Chamcha himself, apparently restored to his old shape, mother-naked but of entirely human aspect and proportions, *humanized* – is there any option but to conclude? – by the fearsome concentration of his hate" (*SV* 294). Therefore, his learning "the power of hatred" (*SV* 401) proves "therapeutic and liberating" for Saladin (Walker 359).

We shall briefly return to Saladin's double Gibreel, as

> *The Satanic Verses* is the story of two painfully divided selves. In the case of one, Saladin Chamcha, the division is secular and societal: he is torn, to put it plainly, between Bombay and London, between East and West. For the other, Gibreel Farishta, the division is spiritual, a rift in the soul... . The novel is 'about' their quest for wholeness. (Rushdie, "In Good Faith" 397)

Gibreel, having transformed, or believing to have transformed, into the archangel, has to fight with his multiple selves. His division finds expression in his dreams, which leak into reality (cf. *SV* 427). Is he the archangel or the Prophet?

> [I]n these moments it begins to seem that the archangel is actually *inside the Prophet,* I am the dragging in the gut, I am the angel being extruded from the sleeper's navel, I emerge, Gibreel Farishta, while my other self, Mahound, lies *listening,* entranced, I am bound to him, navel to navel, by a shining cord of light, not possible to say which of us is dreaming the other. (*SV* 110)

Another division is that between Gibreel Farishta the actor and Gibreel the angel (cf. Kuortti 140). Gibreel begins "to characterize his 'possessed', 'angel' self as another person: in the Beckettian formula, *Not I. He.* His very own Mr Hyde" (*SV* 340). It becomes obvious that for Gibreel, too, the "division between his different selves begin[s] to take shape in a more pathological way" (Kuortti 140). Eventually, he is diagnosed with paranoid schizophrenia (*SV* 429).

As in Ovid, the metamorphoses in *The Satanic Verses* occur at a moment of crisis while in *Midnight's Children* the question of the homogeneity of the self is directly addressed in a moment of physical transformation that becomes a source of identity crisis for Saleem. When a school accident, in which Saleem loses the tip of his finger, makes a blood transfusion necessary, his blood type reveals that he is not his father's son. In this context, he states the following:

> O eternal opposition of inside and outside! Because a human being, inside himself, is anything but a whole, anything but homogeneous; all kinds of everywhichthing are jumbled up inside him, and he is one person and one min-

> ute and another the next. The body, on the other hand, is homogeneous as anything. Indivisible, a once piece-suit, a sacred temple, if you will. It is important to preserve his wholeness. But the loss of my finger…not to mention the removal of certain hairs from my head has undone all that ... Uncork the body and God knows what you permit to come tumbling out. Suddenly you are forever other than you were…And these, mark you, are only the effects on private life. (*MC* 328)

In this quotation, Saleem addresses the continuity of identity in the context of the wholeness of the body. While Rushdie's characters are often described as generally tending to side with Ovid's view of identity, it seems to be valid to conclude from this quotation that at this point Saleem considers the question of the essence of the self in Lucretius' terms: "suddenly you are forever other than you were" – one's old self dies when the form changes. This is similar to the conclusion that Saladin draws from his physical transformation. Comparable to Saladin's experience, Saleem's mutilations work as a kind of metamorphosis that disrupt the wholeness of his body and lead to a fundamental change in the essence of his self and his identity. The loss of his finger has extensive implications for his understanding of himself. It becomes one of the pivotal events that Brooks calls "climatic moments of coming-to-consciousness about one's identity, about the very order of the moral universe" which is "played out on the body" (21–22).

Saleem sees wholeness as an illusion which can be kept up by living in a whole body. The body is viewed as a shell that prevents the conflicting realities underneath from breaking loose. The body is a safeguard that keeps up the illusion of wholeness and ideally withholds potentially clashing realities. This view becomes evident in the description of other characters as well. Amina is described as looking "still and unchanging although great things [are] happening beneath her skin" (*MC* 82), while in *The Satanic Verses*, Saladin starts to think about Pamela's face as "a saintly mask behind which who knows what worms feasted on rotting meat" (*SV* 402). In Saleem's case, however, this physical wholeness is disrupted – first by the pulling out of his hair, then by the loss of his finger. The effects are "revolutionary" – the physical disruption not only transforms his body, but also his self, his identity (*MC* 328). However, the view of body and identity as presented here is not unambiguous. After all, Saleem at a later point insists that "what you were is forever who you are" (*MC* 513), contrasting previous statements.

In order to understand this volte-face, it is important to consider Saleem's account of his time in the Sundarbans. This phase in his life is equally connected to an identity crisis. As he suffers from amnesia, he loses his identity, his self.[29] Saleem's loss of memory results in a loss of "his link with the past which places him in the social and historical context that outlines his individuality" (Cundy 35) and is accompanied by a loss of feeling – his body becomes "head-to-foot numb" (*MC* 487), "anaesthetized against feelings as well as memories" (*MC* 493). Saleem, who formerly embodied India, "as [his] alternative self ... becomes a soldier in the Pakistani army" (Bassi 55). Kortenaar writes that "the body of the amnesiac seems but an empty shell" (106). Interestingly, however, while Saleem's identity is disrupted and his body becomes numb, the only continuous feature is of a physical nature: the special power of his nose, making him a tracker dog in a unit of the Pakistani army. That Saleem is 'not 'himself' anymore is highlighted by the fact that this account slips into a third person narration as he refers to himself as 'the buddha' during the whole jungle episode. Only when Saleem is bitten by a snake and fighting against the poison in his body is he reconnected to his past and is able to refer to himself in the first person again: "at last *he* relaxed, and the look of milky abstraction was no longer in *his* eyes. *I* was rejoined to the past, jolted into unity by snake poison" (*MC* 508; emphasis added). However, what remains lost to Saleem is his first name: "the buddha had forgotten his name" (*MC* 509).

Since we have seen that according to Locke a person's identity is defined by the reach of his or her memory, taking in to account the Sundarban chapter of *Midnight's Children* seems valuable. That memory is indeed an important component of a person's self is also Saleem's belief, who claims that "morality, judgment, character…it all starts with memory" (*MC* 292). This is emphasised later, when Saleem calls India the "amnesiac nation", shortly before he, and with him India, burst into six hundred million particles (*MC* 643). In this context it is also important to remark that Saleem does not claim to have an infallible memory. In fact, admitting that he gets historical facts (like Gandhi's death and the date of the first election) wrong

---

29 Saleem's account of his amnesia is ambiguous as he later admits "that amnesia is the kind of gimmick regularly used by our lurid filmmakers" (*MC* 488).

(cf. Rushdie, "Errata"), serves to advise of the subjectivity of memory and history. However, by showing memory as unreliable and at the same time asserting its importance for the constitution of a person's self-identity, attention is brought to the instability and constructedness of identity itself.

To illustrate Saleem's disconnection from his identity, Rushdie uses the image of transparency. The connection of transparency and loss of self is alluded to by Saleem's grandmother, Reverend Mother, when she refers to photographs of Amina as having "tak[en] away pieces" of her, so that she looked so "transparent" that "the writing from the other side [was] coming right through" her face (*MC* 190). She is persuaded that "cameras could steal your soul" (*MC* 133). As Saleem is lost in the Sundarbans and he and his fellow soldiers meet four "identical beauties", this connection is underlined. As they are being seduced by the women, they "becom[e] transparent, ... it [is] possible to see through their bodies, not clearly as yet, but cloudily" (*MC* 512), "so that as their dream-life seeped out of them they became as hollow and translucent as glass" (*MC* 512). The possibility of translucency echoes the threat of losing one's distinctive self. However, "awakened by the shock of translucency" they make their way out of the jungle eventually (*MC* 512-513). The whole episode serves to illustrate the importance of a person's connection to his or her past, and therefore memory, to retain a sense of self-identity. The image of transparency as symbolizing a loss or disruption of identity has also been touched upon in the description of Gibreel's rotting images after leaving India.

To be able to pass the border and return to India, Saleem is made invisible and weightless by Parvati the Witch, one of the children of midnight. Invisibility is connected to the most extreme loss of self, namely death. Saleem becomes, like a ghost, "present, but insubstantial; actual, but without being or weight" (*MC* 532). In Parvati's wicker basket of invisibility, he is close to death, close to fading, but he is saved by his silver spittoon, his link to the past. While in the basket, Saleem goes through another transformation: he learns to feel angry about his burden, about being handcuffed to history. Giving vent to his feelings restores sensation to his body. Similar to the therapeutic effect anger has on Saladin Chamcha, Saleem is "rescued by rebellion from the abstraction of numbness" (*MC* 535). His anger is described as a very physical process, as "eccrine and apocrine glands [pour] forth sweat and stink", as if Saleem tries to "shed [his] fate", his central role in history that brings too much responsibility, "through [his] pores" (*MC* 535).

Saleem is given back his name by Parvati, who recognises him. Her memory of Saleem's Midnight's Children Conference and consequent act of 'narration', restores Saleem to his familiar self, which was lost only temporarily. The importance of names as symbols of identity and its temporality can also be seen from Amina's story (cf. Kuortti 141). She is called Mumtaz until her second husband "rename[s] and reinvent[s] her" (*MC* 85). Saladin and Gibreel change their names, in Saladin's case this marks a conscious attempt to bring his British identity to perfection. In *The Moor's Last Sigh*, Moraes becomes known as 'the hammer' when he uses his deformed hand to beat up Muslims and thereby fulfils his wish to "be a Hammer, not a Moor" (*MLS* 295). These name-changes draw attention to the potential fluidity of identity and to the importance of words in the process. This becomes particularly evident in the controversial brothel episode, which takes place in one of Gibreel's dream sequences. The prostitutes change their names and with their new names take on new personalities until "their previous selves beg[i]n to fade away" (*SV* 382). "'Our names contain our fates' Saleem tells us [*MC* 423], but a change of name ... means that the individual's fate need not be once and forever determined" (Cundy 42).

Instability is not only presented through transformation of individual bodies. Clouds, gods, and cities also change. Metamorphosis is an important theme as a phenomenon of our modern world: human beings themselves as well as their surroundings become unstable (cf. *SV* 6; cf. Rushdie, "Between God and Devil" 94): "London had grown unstable once again ... a city that had lost its sense of itself" (*SV* 320). Jahilia, London's twin city of Gibreel's dreams, is described in those terms: "how did one map a country that blew into a new form everyday" (*SV* 370). Hind, who we encounter in Gibreel's dreams as the "woman who did not change" (*SV* 392) becomes "to be thought of by Jahilians as the embodiment of the city, its living avatar, because they found in her physical unchangingness ... a description of themselves far more palatable than the picture they saw in the mirror of Simbel's crumbling face" (*SV* 361).

An interesting image that occurs frequently in *Midnight's Children* as well as in *The Satanic Verses* is that of 'leaking'. The leaking of Aadam Aziz's religious uncertainty into Saleem is a strikingly visual image (cf. *MC*

382). It implies that boundaries are not static (cf. Kortenaar 217). Thus it is another hint at the fluidity of identity, at the loose boundaries of the self that characterize many of Rushdie's characters. That Aadam Aziz's "inability to follow his own nose dripped into" Saleem (*MC* 94) confirms the same idea while additionally drawing attention to the fact that although Aadam is not Saleem's 'real' grandfather, he does pass on certain characteristics to him. The world the characters live in, just as their identities, is subjected to that idea of fluidity, illustrated for instance as a disease that "leak[s] into history" (*MC* 53). Gibreel's dream world begins to leak into the real world, which shows how his schizophrenia disables him from distinguishing between the two and from forming a clear understanding of his identity (cf. *SV* 427). The image of leaking draws attention to the loose boundaries of selves and underlines the way in which the outside and the inside are connected. Furthermore, it visualizes the ways in which the private and the public can leak into each other and how extrinsic elements can attach themselves to bodies or to selves.

A curious incident that can be seen as exemplary for Rushdie's depictions of identity is Ahmed Sinai's "heartboot" (*MC* 412). "Overfull of hate resentment self-pity grief" his heart becomes swollen and actually changes shape (*MC* 412). A psychological state is translated directly into a physical change, which again leads to a change in character: "Ahmed came to himself under Amina's care, he returned ... to the self that he might always have been" (*MC* 413). This brings us back to the question of essence: by referring to the self that Ahmed might always have been, it is implied that he went through a change of identity due to external circumstances, but that there is an essence that he finds back thanks to his 'heartboot'. In *The Satanic Verses* the issue of temporary dislocation of identity is broached as well. Saladin's father, who is upset by his son's rejection of his roots, exclaims that he has his "soul kept safe, ... here in this walnut-tree" (*SV* 48). The walnut tree is a symbol of this true essence and Mr Chamchawala is convinced that "the devil has only [Saladin's] body" (*SV* 48). He hopes that one day his son will realise this and "claim [his] immortal spirit" (*SV* 48). Mr Chamchawala opposes Saladin's attitude by claiming that there is a true essence that Saladin can eventually return to, one that is separable from his body. The idea of 'displaced' identities or bodies respectively is also treated as a common phenomenon in London. When Gibreel wanders the streets, he encounters a young man looking for someone in a photograph who turns out to be himself. This man is literally a "lost soul", "a Soul in search of its mislaid body, a spectre in desperate need of its lost physical casing - for it is known to archangels that the soul or ka cannot exist (once the golden cord of light linking it to the body is severed) for more than a night and a day" (*SV* 322).

In Ovid, the metamorphosed beings' new forms "more fully express them than their first form" (Warner 4). What then, about Chamcha's devilish and Gibreel's (arch)angelic form? Chamcha is "no longer *[him]self*, or not only", but is he evil (*SV* 256)? The question about the quality of the essence of the self is addressed in the two opposing transformations of Gibreel and Saladin, devil and angel, nevertheless two halves that together seem to form a whole: "Gibreelsaladin Farishtachamcha" (*SV* 5). Saladin's father foreshadows what Saladin comes to believe too, that his transformation is a punishment for his striving to be English. As if predicting Saladin's transformation, he warns him that "a man untrue to himself becomes a two-legged lie, and such beasts are Shaitan's best work" (*SV* 48). The question of the quality of the essence is ubiquitous, but necessarily left unresolved: "[w]hen a man is unsure of his essence, how may he know if he be good or bad?" (*SV* 192).

6.2.4 Self-Reconciliation

Gibreel and Saladin do not only represent two fundamentally different stances on migrancy and integration but also represent "two fundamentally different types of self" (*SV* 427):

> Gibreel, for all his stage-name and performances; and in spite of born-again slogans, new beginnings, metamorphoses; - has wished to remain, to a large degree, continuous - that is, joined to and arising from his past; ... in point of fact, he fears above all things the altered states in which his dreams leak into ... - so that his is still a self which, for our present purposes, we may describe as 'true' ... whereas Saladin Chamcha is a creature of *selected* discontinuities, a *willing* re-invention; his *preferred* revolt against history being what makes him, in our chosen idiom, 'false'? (*SV* 427)

Saladin is the one to act in a truly evil manner by triggering Gibreel's jealousy with his 'satanic' phone calls, which later leads to Alleluia's death as well as Gibreel's suicide (cf. *SV* 444–446), while Gibreel rescues him from a burning building in spite of knowing what Saladin did. However, to label Gibreel or Saladin in either category, good or evil, true or false, would mean to accept those distinctions as "resting ... on the idea of the self as being (ideally) homogenous, non-hybrid, 'pure'" (*SV* 427). That, however, is shown to be "an utterly fantastic notion" and "cannot, must not, suffice" (*SV* 427).[30] The idea of the self as a homogeneous entity is shown to be untenable: "Through the intermingling of Chamcha and Farishta, Rushdie offers a critique of simple dual oppositions such as East and West, true and false, good and evil, and most important, self and other" (Sanga 39). The line that is drawn between binary distinctions is so porous, that "Rushdie is able to present notions of Self and Other ... as dual entities constantly in dialogue with each other" (Sanga 39).

Gibreel's identity is marked by his unwillingness to accept the notion of change and fluidity. "Clarity, clarity, at all costs clarity!" (*SV* 353), is what he demands and what eventually makes him lose control altogether. As his dreams leak into reality, he loses track of who he is. While Chamcha moves from one identity to the other, Gibreel's conflicting selves exist within him simultaneously.

Saladin realises the hybrid nature of his world when watching TV, being confronted with a culture made of mutants, humanoid robots and creatures with metamorphic bodies. He is confronted with a world of mongrels, of transformation, a world in which "lycanthropy was on the increase" and "the genetic possibility of centaurs was being seriously discussed" (*SV* 405). Saladin is reminded of his friend's poem "I Sing The Body Eclectic", and finds the idea of eclecticism "fully representative of the whole" (SV 405).[31] He is reminded of the fictionality of the notion that there is something like the normal, the real. Rushdie writes in "In Good Faith" that *The Satanic Verses*

> celebrates hybridity, impurity, intermingling, the transformation that comes of new and unexpected combinations of human beings, cultures, ideas, poli-

[30] In *Midnight's Children*, an expression of this ambivalence can be seen in the motif of 'snakes and ladders'.

[31] Jumpy Joshi's poem is reminiscent of Walt Whitman's poem "I sing the Body Electric", in which Whitman sees the body "as a *corporeal* symbol of modernity" (Maldonado 15).

tics, movies, songs. It rejoices in mongrelization and fears the absolutism of the Pure ... that is *how newness enters the world.* (394)

Saladin becomes aware of that potential while watching a programme about gardening, where he sees how a cross-bred graft of two different kinds of trees is "growing vigorously out of a piece of English earth" (*SV* 406). "If such a tree were possible", he thinks to himself, "then so was he; he, too, could cohere, send down roots, survive" (*SV* 406). As he tries to get back to his old life, he realises that "he had been living in a state of phoney peace, that the change in him was irreversible ... no matter how assiduously he attempted to re-create his old existence, this was, he now saw, a fact that could not be unmade" (*SV* 418). The 'migrant's double vision', the simultaneous perspectives of an insider and an outsider make the migrant "both the gardener and the garden" (Huddart 116). The migrant is being made by society, but he must also shape it. However, "the notion of a glorious multicultural hybridity is always slightly undermined, and always a little anxious. It is always just possible that the wondrous hybrid will be caught between two (or more) monolithic identities" (Huddart 115).

As for Saladin, he comes to experience a fate similar to that of the protagonist of Apuleius' *The Golden Ass*, whose "true self generates itself in its proper character after undergoing several transformations" (Warner 85). Saladin's body is restored to its former state, however, he must realise that his sense of identity has not remained unscathed. His physical change has enabled him to see reality from the perspective of the 'other' and to profit from the awareness that has come with this experience. Reconciled with his dying father in Bombay, he finds himself at peace with his old selves, "many alternative Saladins - or rather Salahuddins ... which had apparently continued to exist, perhaps in the parallel universes of quantum theory" (*SV* 524). He realises that his old self has not been chopped down with the walnut tree, but manages to unite and balance his "conflicting selves jostling and joggling within these bags of skin" (*SV* 519). They are all within him, inhabiting the same body. By returning to his roots, "he makes himself whole" (Rushdie, "In Good Faith" 398). Therefore, in spite of all the postmodern uncertainties traceable in the novel, the protagonist ultimately embraces a certain kind of continuity.[32] Gibreel, on the other hand, unable to accept any compromises in his identity, commits suicide: "The contrast between Gibreel at the beginning and the end of the novel suggests that his restlessness and his desire to reinvent his identity, coupled with his inability to do so in a final sense, lead to his suicide" (Huddart 114). It turns out that his 'almost' dying twice does not 'add up' after all, and that "to be born again, first [he has] to die" (*SV* 3). Today, we must accept "uncertainty as the only constant" (Rushdie, "In Good Faith" 405).

In *Midnight's Children,* Saleem goes through a comparably dramatic journey. Similar to Saladin's experience, after a tentative rejection of the Ovidian viewpoint, he comes to embrace the idea of an immutable essence. When Saleem loses his memory and consciousness, he loses "the glue of personality" (*MC* 490); the connection between past and present that is a precondition for a coherent identity. At the same time, the disconnection from that consciousness is proof of his homogeneity to him, as, when he regains his memory and thereby his connection to his past, he realises that "what you were is forever who you are" (*MC* 513). He is finally able to answer the question of who he is:

> I am the sum total of everything that went before me, of all I have been seen done, of everything done-to-me. I am everyone everything whose being-in-the-world affected was affected by mine ... each 'I', every one of the now-six-hundred-million-plus of us, contains a similar multitude. I repeat for the last time: to understand me you'll have to swallow a world. (*MC* 535)

This can be read as an acceptance of himself as a private individual: "He is no longer the mirror of the nation, single and sovereign, who resists his dissolution in the many, but is now a pluriform and contingent self made up of many" (Kortenaar 78). Saleem still "claims links between the outside world and himself" (Kuortti 68), an interconnectedness with others, but he does not insist on his centrality to India as a whole.

In *The Moor's Last Sigh,* a self-reconciliation does seem to take place. Moor's inner conflict arises, as outlined above, due to the felt incongruence of body and true self. One reason for Moor to join Mumbai's Axis is that he can be himself, that he does not have to conceal his deformed hand and that

---

32 When Saladin's father dies and Saladin sees his father's dead body being treated by mullah "as a commonplace thing" he is appalled (*SV* 532). This can be read as another confirmation of the rejection of Lucretius' views on body and soul.

he is surrounded by men with peculiar bodies, as for example the Tin-Man, "a man, but with metal parts" (*MLS* 301). Moor's left hand, which he is forced to make his writing hand, is finally substituted by his right hand, his 'hammer', which in Mumbai's Axis is "set free to write the story of [his] life" (*MLS* 305). When Moor joins MA, Fielding asks him: "My zombie, my hammer: are you for us or against us, will you be righteous or will you be leftous?" (*MLS* 295). Moor chooses the "righteous" path and becomes a "man of violence" (MLS 367), using his powerful right hand as a henchman. However, he comes to regret this period of his life later. Determined to kill his boss Fielding, it is significantly his left hand that deals the deadly stroke, "that same left hand which [he] had to force myself, all [his] life, and against [his] nature, to learn how to use" (*MLS* 367). "What triumphs over Fielding's superior physical strength is precisely Moraes's lettered hand" (Burningham 130). In the end, Moor realises the power of narration and comes to understand his left hand as a more powerful way to 'write the story of his life'. His 'lettered hand' allows him to save his life by enabling him to write.

6.3 Secret Identities

"I was mild-mannered Clark Kent protecting my secret identity; but what on earth was that?", asks Saleem (*MC* 212). As a child, he is overwhelmed by his family's high expectations in him. His father is convinced that "what's in store" for him are "great deeds, a great life" while his grandmother tells him that he can be "better than anyone in the whole wide world" (*MC* 210). A way of dealing with this pressure and his fear of meaninglessness, which to Saleem comes to life as a "shapeless animal" and a "creature" (*MC* 210), is to escape into the world of fairytales. The tales of Eastern as well as Western origin, "Hatim Tai and Batman, Superman and Sindbad, helped to get [Saleem] through the nearlynine years" (*MC* 210). While his friends from school seem to know exactly where their lives will lead them, Saleem feels like he has to protect his secret identity, even before knowing what it is. After the "accident in the washing-chest" that awakens his powers, Saleem finds the answer. His secret identity becomes the power of his nose, which makes telepathic journeys and eventually the Midnight's Children Conference possible. After sharing the secret of the voices in his head with his family and receiving a punitive beating on his ear, Saleem is reminded "of the need for secrecy" (*MC* 234), and continues to fear the revelation of his "true nature" (*MC* 323). He becomes Clark Kent, in possession of super powers which are kept a secret. As Saleem's secret identity rests in his nose, the 'secret' of Moor's identity, his "true self" is "contained in that deformed limb which [he] had thrust for too long into the depths of [his] clothing" (*MLS* 295).

Similar to the references to Superman in *Midnight's Children*, the aspect of secret identities is introduced by means of cartoon figures in *The Moor's Last Sigh*. When Vasco Miranda first appears at the Zogoiby's mansion, he is hired to paint the children's nursery. The cartoons he paints on the walls to give the kids their "paradise" come to mean much more. They signify "the notion he implanted in all of us through the pictures on our walls: the notion, that is, of the secret identities" (*MLS* 152). Here, the reference to secret identity expresses the idea that "beneath every hero there is a normal person" (Kuortti 199). Moor comes to identify with the superheroes on the pictures due to his 'special' physique. Although he does not see himself as a superhero, he shares a superhero's "yearn for normality": "I was exceptional all right, and had no desire to be" (*MLS* 152). Inspired by the paintings on the wall, Moraes sets out to create "a secret identity of [his] very own" (*MLS* 152). His "Slomo" identity is only "the most visible of [his] layers of disguise" (*MLS* 153) - moving in slow motion and talking more slowly can be seen as Moor's attempt to counteract the speed of his physical 'evolution' (*MLS* 152-153). A lot of his true feelings are concealed: "The first lessons of my Paradise were educations in metamorphosis and disguise" (*MLS* 154). With Miranda Vasco's help, Moor establishes yet another secret identity: one that provides him with a powerful and invisible third hand. He comes to believe that it is his third hand that changes the paintings on the wall over night and that he can alter his surroundings magically. Possibly it is this creative third hand, which enables him to write down his story toward the end of his life. Vasco Miranda, too, is hiding a secret that he shares with Moraes. Like him, Miranda has to live his life in a hurry, as a "needle lost inside him" could kill him at any moment (*MLS* 154). Moor understands the metaphorical nature of the needle story. While wondering why Vasco does not get it removed, he understands that it is a part of himself, a part of his identity. The needle makes him what he is. Here, the secret of identity and personality is put into the form of a metaphor again, a metaphor that is literalised when Vasco is killed in the very end of the novel by the metaphorical lost needle (*MLS* 432).[33]

In the style of the analysis of *The Moor's Last Sigh* above, secret identities shall be seen as another expression of the palimpsestic form of identities. In this context, one can perceive a secret identity as the bottom layer of a palimpsest. As has been established, Moor's identity is marked by the discrepancy between his inside and his outside. His secret identity is the one that no-one can see: the ten year-old child as opposed to the twenty year-old young man. Vasco Miranda, when talking about art, remarks that "the real is always hidden - isn't it?" (*MLS* 174) - thus likening art and identity as fundamentally palimpsestic. The foremost example that illustrates the fictionality as well as the dangers of layered identities is the character of Uma - Moor's lover. She can be seen as someone who comes to lack a secret identity, as she can no longer distinguish between her own identities, both real and fictional:

> It was possible that [Uma] no longer had a clear sense of an 'authentic' identity that was independent of these performances, and this existential confusion had begun to spread beyond the borders of her own self and to infect, like a disease, all those with whom she came into contact. (*MLS* 266)

If a secret identity is to be equated with an authentic identity, then Uma does not possess one. Her "existential confusion" seems to have pathological consequences. Private eye Dom Minto finds out that Uma has been lying about her origins. She "was not from Gujarat but from Maharashtra - the other half of the divided self of the former Bombay State" (*MLS* 265). This illustrates not only of the partition of the Indian states, but also of Uma's mind - divided in multiple selves she seems to have lost track of where she really belongs. Uma's "very embodiment of plural identity reverses its value - a perception Moor records as a 'bitter parable' in which the 'polarities of good and evil were reversed'" (Grant 118).

Moares' father Abraham, on the other hand, creates his secret identity very consciously. Like Saleem, he uses a "mild-mannered secret identity to mask his covert super-nature" (*MLS* 179). However, Abraham's disguise,

---

33 The reader is left with two possible causes for Vasco Miranda's death: he might have been killed by the metaphorical needle lost inside his body, or by the 'literal' needle standing for his drug addiction.

his "overneath", is for him a means to rule the underworld and uphold his numerous criminal activities (*MLS* 180).

In *The Satanic Verses* the idea of secret identities must be seen as a consequence of migrancy: migrants become disguises, "false descriptions to counter falsehoods invented about [them], concealing for reasons of security [their] secret selves" (*SV* 49). Here, the migrant's identity is seen as layered as a form of defence mechanism.

7. Powerful Bodies

Bodies in Rushdie's writing are often shown as possessing a life of their own – their own will, as has been observed in the context of Chamcha's 'treacherous' body parts. They can become independent from the self: "But now my nose has had enough; staging its own, unprompted revolt against the grasping thumb-and-forefinger, it unleashes a weapon of its own" (*MC* 321) – here Saleem's body parts are fighting out a battle his consciousness does not seem to be part of, but which turns out to have significant consequences (the 'accident' marks the beginning of his telepathic abilities). Another context in which the body or body parts act independently is that of sexual excitement. One example can be found in Methwold's and Vanita's affair. When Vanita is "alone with the centre-parting", which has already been singled out as the symbol of Methwold's power, she feels it "exert a pull on her fingers that was impossible to resist, and as Methwold sat immobile in a cane chair ... she found herself approaching him ... felt fingers touching hair; found centre-parting; and began to rumple it up" (*MC* 136-137). However, as Kortenaar points out, this independence can pose a threat to the self (cf. 101). In the Sundarbans, Saleem and his fellow soldiers meet four girls "without names or selves" to whom they almost lose their selves (Kortenaar 101-102). As they make love, "eight arms [are] twined with eight, eight legs [are] linked with eight legs" (*MC* 511). By counting all of them together, ignoring "the integrity of the individual self", the imminent threat of the loss of self is underlined (Kortenaar 102).

In *The Moor's Last Sigh,* sexual agitation leads to the mind losing power over the body: "for my body knew what I did not ... my limbs began to act ... quite independently of my mind" (*MLS* 190). An interesting example is also that of Ahmed's physical change that occurs after his marriage to Amina. At that time, she is still in love with her first husband Nadir Khan. Here, his body acts independently of his mind (or rather of his will), but seemingly on command of Amina's unconscious will:

> Under the influence of a painstaking magic so obscure that Amina was probably unaware of working it, Ahmed Sinai found his hair thinning and what was left becoming lank and greasy; he discovered that he was willing to let it grow until it began to spread over the tops of his ears. Also, his stomach be-

> gan to spread, until it became the yielding, squashy belly in which I would so often be smothered and which none of us, consciously at any rate, compared to the pudginess of Nadir Khan. (*MC* 88)

In this case, the seizing control over another's body makes up for a lost love. Mian Abdullah's political popularity and persuasiveness is equally illustrated in the power he exerts over others' bodies: his hum has "the ability of inducing erections in anyone within its vicinity ... Nadir Khan, as his secretary, [is] attacked constantly by his master's vibratry quirk, and his ears jaw penis [are] forever behaving according to the dictates of the Hummingbird (*MC* 55).

However, bodies are also shown as weapons in characters' fight to remain autonomous. When Reverend Mother and Aadam Aziz fight over her firing their children's religious education teacher, Naseem punishes him by denying him food. As he grows thinner and thinner his body becomes "a battlefield and each day a piece of it was blasted away" (*MC* 51). Saleem recalls his grandparents' fight as a "war of starvation", which is reminiscent of Gandhi's non-violent means of protest. Here, Aadam becomes a Gandhi-like figure. In the story of Zafar, Saleem's cousin, and his fiancée, we encounter two characters who represent both powerful and powerless bodies. Zafar is "doomed" by incontinence (*MC* 465) – his lack of control over his bodily functions denies him a great part of his identity. His own father rejects him and chooses Saleem as his son. His fiancée, on the other hand, "resolves not to arrive at puberty", as she tries to avoid physical intimacy with Zafar (*MC* 464). Unable to object to the marriage, her body becomes her only means of resistance.

8. Body as Text

While in feminist theory the body is treated as "a problematic text" in that it is a system of signs "which stand for and express relations of power" (Turner 27), the understanding of the body as text shall be considered in a literal way in the context of Rushdie's writing. Once again Saleem serves as the most obvious example. He describes his pre-natal growth in terms of a linguistic metaphor that allows a literal 'body as text' image:

> What had been (at the beginning) no bigger than a full stop had expanded into a comma, a word, a sentence, a paragraph, a chapter; now it was bursting into more complex developments, becoming, one might say, a book - perhaps an encyclopaedia - even a whole language. (*MC* 133)

Saleem's body, here literally consisting of textual symbols, must be seen as text in so far as it contains the ever-expanding history of India, while his body becomes the script of his private history. Furthermore, his story, that is also the story of his body, becomes quite literally the book the reader holds in his hands. One might call this what Peter Brooks terms "narrative aesthetics of embodiment, where meaning and truth are made carnal" (Brooks 21). Saleem's body is "made a signifier", a "place on which messages are written" (Brooks 21). It is a site of cultural inscription as well as a personal 'battlefield'. His bodily inscriptions "not only serve to recognize and identify", they can also be seen as designating "the body's passage into the realm of the letter, into literature: the bodily mark is in some manner a 'character', a 'hieroglyph', a sign that can eventually, at the right moment of the narrative, be read" (Brooks 22).

As he gets older, the inscriptions on his body accumulate. Saleem's description of his physical features is frequently given in the form of an enumeration, which becomes longer and longer in the course of his story. In the beginning of his autobiography, Saleem describes his baby-self as lying "horn-templed, cucumber-nosed" in his crib (*MC* 182). By the time he is about thirty years old, the list is somewhat longer: he is "nine-fingered, horn-templed, monk's-tonsured, stain-faced, bow-legged, cucumber-nosed, castrated, and now prematurely aged" (*MC* 624). All these features are read by Saleem as the marks of history, while, at the same time, they are signs pointing to his experiences of personal crises. The body as text becomes more complex and expands, until in the end, Saleem has become a "human being to whom history could do no more" (*MC* 624-625). In this context, the term 'felt history' first used by John Burt Foster Jr. comes to mind. 'Felt history'

> must be distinguished from official history with its attention to leaders, its overview of events, or its analysis of underlying trends. And it should also be distinguished from emotions or feelings, since history's psychological effects are usually less dramatic and revealing than its immediate feel, *its physical impact on the body and the senses*. In essence, then, felt history refers to the eloquent gestures and images with which a character or lyric persona registers the direct pressure of events. (Foster Jr. 273; emphasis added)

This analysis is applicable to *Midnight's Children*, as well *The Satanic Verses*. Here, history's effects are mainly connected to the processes at work in postcolonial societies. While physical effects might not be more dramatic, they are indeed much more revealing than psychological processes, especially since bodily changes might force repressed psychological dilemmas into the person's consciousness to begin with, as in the case of Chamcha's metamorphosis.

Saleem's body is being read by his teacher Zagallo by means of what he calls "human geography" (*MC* 321). Reading Saleem's face as a map of India he translates the stains on Saleem's temples as representing Pakistan while "thees birthmark on the right ear is the East Wing; and these horrible stained left cheek, the West!" (*MC* 321). Saleem's body becomes literally a map; his imperfections come to represent geographical entities. Saleem not only *contains* the multitudes of India inside his body metaphorically (which leads to his cracking up quite literally), but he also represents the subcontinent's geography externally.

Another example, which shows how text can quite literally turn into flesh and vice versa, is the episode in which Reverend Mother, Saleem's grandmother, stops talking. As a consequence, her body swells up, becomes bigger and bigger, as "the unspoken words inside her ... [blow] her up" (*MC* 74). The unspoken words do not disappear but are literally incarnated so that, as if to encompass them, her skin becomes "dangerously stretched" (*MC* 74). When she speaks again for the first time three years later, the words that her body has kept safe come pouring out, leaving it permanently altered: "Three years of words poured out of her (but her body, stretched by the exigencies of storing them, did not diminish)" (*MC* 76). This is similar to what happens to Aadam, Shiva's and also Saleem's son, who refuses to talk or cry as a child, almost choking on "the torrential vomit of pent-up sound" (*MC* 591). Both images can be seen as a foreshadowing of Saleem's final disintegration; his body is overwhelmed with the text he has to incorporate in the course of his lifetime and cannot make it flesh anymore.

Text imagined as body is an idea that can also be found in *The Moor's Last Sigh*. As Gonzalez writes, the text can here be seen as a body:

> A 'last sigh', a 'breath', the text is 'ex-haled', dragged out of the confines of itself as fixed identity ... so that, like Moraes, it becomes 'weightless, floating free of burdens'. Breathing itself 'out' as a radical but fragile 'body' of creation undergoing constant metamorphosis ... its final refuge is inevitably in the release of sleep/death. (132)

Metafictional strategies become apparent, as *The Moor's Last Sigh* is also written in the form of an autobiography, constantly reminding the reader that what he reads is the product of Moraes' creative endeavour. Gonzalez illustrates how this likens the text to a body as "the interest of the story is displaced towards its existence as a creative process, a painful procedure, in which the text, akin to a suffering body, distorts itself so as to not remain a dead letter" (136). Just as Saleem encourages the readers (or listeners) to imagine themselves "inside [him] somehow", to look out through his eyes, to hear the noise and the voices (*MC* 235), Moor makes the reader "the companions of [the text's] torments" (Gonzalez 136). It becomes a "body both endomorphic and ectomorphic" as it "moves permanently between inside and out, malfunctioning on purpose, like the valve of a fast-beating heart, when the regulation of the blood flow is no longer under control and the pulse gets carried away" (Gonzalez 139).

As Moor promises from the start that what lies ahead is a story of ruined limbs, this pledge is given a twofold meaning in the course of the novel. After Aurora accidentally drives over Lambajan's leg, "subtracting a leg and therefore his future", she seeks "fiercely to enlarge him again, providing him with a new uniform, a new job, a new leg, a new identity" (*MLS* 135). The loss of body parts is therefore intrinsically connected to a change of identity, subsequently making Moor's story about ruined limbs one about identity as well. Lambajan makes up a story of how an elephant bit off his leg, instead of telling how he really lost his leg. Moor calls his story a "loss-of-limb" tale as he wonders how many of those "were wandering around the city, attaching themselves to amputor or amputee" (*MLS* 297). The stories people make up are seen as becoming part of their bodies, as completing themselves, seemingly randomly. This is connected to identity, which is written and rewritten much like text. Moor himself calls his old life an "amputated limb", thus allowing for his own story to be read as a 'loss-of-limb' tale (*MLS* 309).

9. Writing Identity

"Philosophy, psychoanalysis, and the neurosciences have demonstrated that our identity depends on (or coincides with) a narrative vision of our existence, on an endless making and remaking of personal stories" (Bassi 54). As two of the novels under discussion are written as fictional autobiographies, the idea of 'writing identity' by writing one's life story is significant. Writing "involves putting a certain distance between ourselves and the contexts that define our identity" (Chambers 10). Aruna Srivastava calls the impulse to narrate and to create stories "an impulse to order, to make sense of an apparently chaotic world, to create a coherent sense of self" (qtd. in Smale 78). As has been established, identity is constructed and "narrative is the medium through which that construction is realized"; the importance of alterity remains important also in this context: "If we tell ourselves and others the story of who we are, we also tell those of who we are not" (Schick 21-22).

In *Midnight's Children*, writing seems to go beyond that. "I have no hope of saving my life, nor can I count on having even a thousand nights and a night. I must work faster, faster than Sheherazade, if I am to end up meaning - yes, meaning - something", Saleem informs the reader, thus expressing the urgency of his literary undertaking (*MC* 7). Meaninglessness is what Saleem seems to fear the most. Writing enables him to make sense of his life. "In fact the *raison d'etre* of the narrative", writes Bode, "is the construction of a continuous identity against all appearances" (31). Saleem and his midnight's children, first seen as the hope of India, fail in uniting the nation. Writing his own story as intrinsically connected to India's is his attempt at a "unified narrative of the nation" (Heffernan 475). While memory is certainly a key to constructing narratives of identity, it is also important to keep in mind that narration is not just a reproduction but a way of establishing new meaning. Benedict Anderson points out the impossibility of remembering identity, which therefore must be narrated (cf. 204). "The need for a narrative of identity" is engendered by the need for an experience of continuity (Anderson 205). While this is true for nations as well as for individuals, the difference between the two is that "nations ... have no clearly identifiable births" (Anderson 205). In *Midnight's Children*, the parallel urge for a narration of both nation and individual is increased by the simultaneous births of Saleem and India. As Saleem is stuck in the divide between public and private, he "tries to reconcile the sense of national community with his particular life through a coherent narrative of his private self that will mirror perfectly that of his community" (Heffernan 475-476). Writing becomes the "act of imaginary reunification" that makes a nation (Hall, "Cultural Identity" 224).

Saleem, just like Oskar in *The Tin Drum*, seems to have "an artistic compulsion to seek [his] own identity through, in Stephen Kellman's phrase, a 'self-begetting' novel"[34] (Merivale 330). That his story is being heard is necessary for meaning to enfold and thus to save Saleem from meaninglessness and disintegration. When Padma, his "necessary ear" is absent, he feels "cracks widening down the length of [his] body" (*MC* 206). But, in Heffernan's words, "how tenable is India's nationalist slogan 'unity in diversity' that Saleem tries so desperately to adhere in his narrative of independence?" (475). As Saleem slowly acknowledges the absurdity of his claim on centrality within Indian history, the cracks on his body widen. He writes his autobiography as a form of defence against the disintegration of his own body. Writing becomes an attempt at creating a coherent personal identity as well as a means of ensuring physical integrity. In this way he compares himself to Sheherezade who, like him, narrates in order to postpone her death.

Saleem, who has become impotent, first emotionally, then physically, can be seen as positioning "textual production against biological procreation as a superior method of national formation" (Kane 97). His sexual impotency is ironically contrasted with his "desire to 'give birth' to the nation" (Heffernan 485). While both Saleem and Moor, are "to remain procreatively impotent, ... [they are] able to turn [their] impotence into creative strength" (Kuortti 80). In this sense, we are led back to the previous chapter, as the text becomes a surrogate body.

The form of *Midnight's Children* makes clear that an attempt at narrating a coherent identity cannot be entirely successful, not necessarily because of errors that are ascribed to Saleem's faulty memory but because of the ambition to encompass all of reality that can never be fulfilled: "Is this an In-

34 Self-begetting novels are stories, which narrate the story of how the protagonist becomes an artist.

dian disease, this urge to encapsulate the whole of reality? Worse: am I infected, too?" (*MC* 97). Saleem digresses from his story and asks himself whether he would end at a different place if he were to start writing from the beginning. As Saleem and the nation become more and more fragmentary, "his chronicle alone remains as the material container of national meaning, for the nation dies with Saleem's body" (Kane 96).

As with *Midnight's Children, The Moor's Last Sigh* does not only encompass one individual life but also seeks to 'narrate the nation', in Homi Bhabha's words (cf. Trivedi 154). Here too, the narrator's physical integrity is dependent on his writing. Truly a Sheherazade, Moraes must produce a piece of writing every day to amuse his persecutor Vasco Miranda, who threatens to kill him. In writing, Moor finally achieves what he dreamed of for so long: "So, in writing, I must peel off history, the prison of the past" (*MLS* 136). The Moor, caught in the "prison" of his body (*MLS* 190), has dreamed of being flayed, of peeling off his skin and with it history. Thereby, he can become free of societal expectations connected with his body, and, more importantly, of history as it is written on his body. This is ultimately his motive for writing the autobiography, that is, for continuing after Vasco Miranda's death. Although at first Moor is forced to write to save his life, it must nevertheless be seen as an attempt at identity formation.

Moor's statement, "I sigh therefore I am", shows that continuity is expressed in the act of breathing: "In the beginning and unto the end was and is the lung" (*MLS* 53). While it is "easier to breathe in than out", Moraes insists that one must "inhale the world and breathe out meaning" (*MLS* 54). Having escaped from Vasco Miranda's clutches and saved the papers on which the story of his life is written, Moor manages to nail his theses to the doors, fulfilling his "last purpose" (*MLS* 433). His story is his last sigh, the meaning he exhales, and can thus be seen as a successful act of identity narration.

As a final remark it is important to mention the parallels between form and content in the novels under discussion. Metamorphosis, which has been established as a main theme within the story, can also be connected to the act of writing. According to Warner "as a literary figure, [metamorphosis] refuses to settle between the states of metaphorical evocation to actual description and embodies the condition of writing itself" (16). Rushdie himself envisions the metamorphoses at work in *The Satanic Verses* as going beyond the physical transformations of its main protagonists: "I thought the book itself was conceived as one which constantly metamorphosed. It keeps turning into another kind of book" (Rushdie, "Salman Rushdie Talks" 216). Similarly, Moor's premature ageing disorder gives the novel a formal and stylistic urgency, and Saleem's non-linear narration digresses profusely, as he believes that "to understand [him] you'll have to swallow a world" (*MC* 535).

10. Conclusion

The body is only one of the many angles from which the characters of Rushdie's novels can be observed. However, it proves to be a productive one. The body serves as a magnifying glass that allows a clearer insight into socio-political issues as well as psychological ones by means of a common referent. The body is thus always inextricably linked to the themes of identity and the perception of reality. In a world of postmodern uncertainty, in which Rushdie's characters as well as his readers find themselves, the body is a necessary signifier. Foucault claims that "nothing in man - not even his body - is sufficiently stable to serve as a basis for self-recognition or for understanding other men" (qtd. Hall, "Introduction" 11). In Rushdie's writing, however, we can see the body obtain meaning as a signifier. Even if it is an inherently unstable one, as can be seen especially in *The Satanic Verses* and *Midnight's Children*, it remains a source of meaning (cf. Hall, "Introduction" 11). In the novels discussed in this paper, bodies undergo meaningful transformations, leading to a questioning of certainties, which proves fundamental for the understanding and formation of the self. That the body is not stable is therefore a consequence as well as a precondition of reality. Its instability becomes a symptom of societal or cultural conditions, just as it enforces an engagement with that reality.

In the theoretical part of this paper, the function of the body in literature as suggested by Deborah Lupton has been expounded. It has been found to reveal "the psychological development of the characters"; ill bodies were displayed as a "test of the moral fibre of the afflicted individual or society, exposing their true nature" (Lupton 51). These ideas have proven to be relevant for Rushdie's usage of the body. Saladin Chamcha's disfigured body allows insight into processes of 'othering' in London's multicultural society, while Moor's ageing disorder can be read as an extreme manifestation of accelerated history. The body politic metaphor, that was originally used to express unity, comes to depict societal realities such as a sense of fragmentation. However, while these are prime examples in which the body is employed, its importance does not end here. The body is not only significant as a metaphorical mirror, it is also crucial insofar as it bridges the gap between public and private, which makes a reflection possible.

Even more importantly, the body is not just shown to be a reflection, a passive expression of identity formation or deformation, it is also an active constituent. Bodies and body parts are portrayed as having a will and a life of their own, which can make for humorous passages, but such a portrayal is also shown as having dramatic consequences. It is often the incongruence between body and (perceived) self that forces the protagonists to make sense not only of themselves, 'their selves', but also of their bodies. In the novels under discussion, bodies shape destinies and demand to be heard. Synnott's assertion, that "the identity of body and self is total" (2) is confirmed as well as challenged in Salman Rushdie's novels. The protagonists' postmodern engagement in formations and deformations of identity is accompanied by a constant renegotiation of the relationship between body and self. In their quest for wholeness the protagonists go through physical odysseys, which, in the case of *Midnight's Children* and *The Moor's Last Sigh,* eventually lead to the narration of their stories.

The body and the role it plays in the processes of identity formation is considered in numerous disciplines, some of which have been touched on in the beginning of this paper. It would prove interesting to widen the understanding of specifically Eastern concepts of corporeality and compare them to Western notions in a more direct manner. Rushdie's writing has widely been regarded as an expression of hybridity in the depiction of his characters as well as in the novels' form and intertexts. Considerable academic attention has been paid to intertexts by authors such as Sterne, Marquez, Grass, Gogol, and Kafka, which are described by Rushdie as having had a fundamental influence on his writing (cf. Rushdie, "Imaginative Maps" 22), an influence that can be recognized in his depiction of bodies. Indian or Eastern texts, however, could be scrutinized in greater detail in this context. Outstanding works such as the great Indian epics and collections of stories, such as *The Arabian Nights,* come to mind.

It has become clear that identity formation in Rushdie's novels is marked by a constant discrepancy between purity and hybridity. One cannot reduce the core of identity to true or false, good or bad, as identities which remain static and renounce heterogeneity are shown as being dangerous in themselves. The threat of purity is externalised in *The Satanic Verses,* however, in *The Moor's Last Sigh,* the threat of fundamentalism in a hybrid and pluralist society is even more strikingly represented, as Moor's city of 'mongrel-joy' is blown apart.

In his later novels, such as *The Ground Beneath Her Feet*, published in 1999, Rushdie moves away from India and further into a more globalized and Western setting. The themes of migration and metamorphosis are of central importance to the aforementioned novel as becomes clear when considering its narrator's thoughts:

> Metamorphosis ... is what supplants our need for the divine... I'm talking now not about the ordinary, quotidian changes that are the stuff of modern life ... but about a deeper, more shocking capacity, which kicks in only under extreme pressure. When we are faced with the Immense. At such a hinge moment we can occasionally mutate into another, final form, a *form beyond metamorphosis.* (461)

The crises that the protagonists of *Midnight's Children, The Satanic Verses* and *The Moor's Last Sigh* undergo are all accompanied by a physical change, a dramatization of the inner processes of change. It might prove enlightening to illuminate the aspect of identity formation as an experience of katabasis in Rushdie's later novels. How are identity conflicts dramatised in these works? Like *The Ground Beneath Her Feet, Fury* (2001) is set in the United States. Expanding the analysis attempted in this paper to a discussion of Rushdie's recent novels could prove productive, particularly as Rushdie draws parallels between India and America (cf. Rushdie, "The Moor's Last Sigh" 205). In a society in which "the American self [is] reconceiving itself in mechanical terms", its relationship to the body would have to be further scrutinized (Rushdie, *Fury* 183).

In the realm of literature, a concept discussed in philosophy, psychology or religion can obtain new meaning altogether. Literature should not only be seen as an expression, but also as an appropriation of culture. In Rushdie's novels, we are confronted with an understanding of the body that makes its own claims for reality. A consideration of body *and* self leaves us with a clearer understanding of how the questions of identity are addressed by the characters of the novels and ultimately by Rushdie himself.

Bibliography

Agnew, Vijay. Introduction. *Diaspora, Memory and Identity: A Search for Home*. By Agnew. Toronto: Toronto UP, 2005. 3–18.

Alter, Joseph S. "Body, Text, Nation: Writing the Physically Fit in Post-Colonial India." *Confronting the Body: The Politics of Physicality in Colonial and Post-Colonial India*. Ed. James H. Mills and Satadru Sen. London: Anthem Press, 2004. 16–38.

"Analogy of the Body Politic." *Dictionary of the History of Ideas*. 15 November 2007 <http://etext.lib.virginia.edu/cgi-local/DHI/dhi.cgi?id=dv1-11>.

Anderson, Benedict. *Imagined Communities: Reflections on the Origin and Spread of Nationalism*. London: Verso, 1996.

Ashcroft, Bill, Gareth Griffiths, and Helen Tiffin. *The Empire Writes Back: Theory and Practice in Postcolonial Literatures*. London: Routledge, 1989.

---. "Hybridity." *Key Concepts in Postcolonial Studies*. London: Routledge, 1998.

---. "Mimicry." *Key Concepts in Postcolonial Studies*. London: Routledge, 1998.

---. "Postcolonial Body." *Key Concepts in Postcolonial Studies*. London: Routledge, 1998.

Assmann, Aleida, and Heidrun Friese, eds. Einleitung. *Identitäten*. By Assmann and Friese. Frankfurt a. M.: Suhrkamp, 1999. 11–23.

Ball, John Clement. *Satire and the Postcolonial Novel: V.S. Naipul, Chinua Achebe, Salman Rushdie*. London: Routledge, 2003.

Bassi, Shaul. "Salman Rushdie's Special Effects." *Coterminous Worlds: Magical Realism and Contemporary Post-Colonial Literature in English*. Ed. Elsa Linguanti, Francesco Casotti and Carmen Concilio. Amsterdam: Rodopi, 1999. 47–69.

Bauman, Zygmunt. "From Pilgrim to Tourist." *Questions of Cultural Identity*. Ed. Stuart Hall and Paul du Gay. London: Sage, 1996. 18–36.

Best, Shaun. *A Beginner's Guide to Social Theory*. London: Sage, 2003.

Bhabha, Homi K. "Dissemination: Time, Narrative and the Margins of the Modern Nation." *The Location of Culture*. London: Routledge, 1994.139–170.

---. "How Newness Enters the World: Postmodern Space, Postcolonial Times and the Trials of Cultural Translation." *The Location of Culture*. London: Routledge, 1994. 212–235.

---. "Introduction: Locations of Culture." *The Location of Culture*. London: Routledge, 1994. 1–18.

---. "Of Mimicry and Man: The Ambivalence of Colonial Discourse." *October* 28 (Spring, 1984): 125–133.

Bode, Christoph. "Plus ca change... - Cultural Continuities and Discontinuities and the Negotiation of Alterity." *Metamorphosis: Structures of Cultural Transformations*. Ed. Jürgen Schlaeger and Winfried Fluck. Tübingen: Gunter Narr Verlag, 2005. 27–38.

Booker, M. Keith. "Beauty and the Beast: Dualism as Despotism in the Fiction of Salman Rushdie." *ELH* 57.4 (Winter 1990): 977–997.

Brennan, Timothy. *Salman Rushdie and the Third World: Myths of the Nation*. Basingstoke: Macmillan, 1989.

Brigg, Peter. "Salman Rushdie's Novels: the Disorder in Fantastic Order." *Reading Rushdie: Perspectives on the Fiction of Salman Rushdie*. Ed. D.M. Fletcher. Amsterdam: Rodopi, 1994. 173–185.

Brooks, Peter. *Body Work: Objects of Desire in Modern Narrative*. Cambridge: Harvard UP, 1993.

Butcher, Melissa. *Transnational Television, Cultural Identity and Change: When STAR Came to India*. New Delhi: Sage, 2003.

Burningham, Bruce. "Salman Rushdie, Author of the Captive's Tale." *Journal of Commonwealth Literature* 38 (2003): 113–133.

Chambers, Ian. *Migrancy, Culture, Identity*. London: Routledge. 1994.

Charmaz, Kathy. "The Body, Identity, and Self: Adapting to Impairment." *Sociological Quarterly* 36.4 (1995): 657–680.

Cundy, Catherine. *Salman Rushdie*. Manchester: Manchester UP, 1996.

Davies, Tony and Robbie B.H. Goh. "Introduction: Britishness and the Construction of Postcolonial Identities." *Postcolonial Cultures and Literatures:*

Modernity and the (Un)Commonwealth. Ed. Andrew Benjamin, Tony Davies and Robbie B.H. Goh. New York: Peter Lang, 2002.

Degler, Frank, and Christian Kohlroß. *Epochen/Krankheiten.* St. Ingbert: Röhrig Universitätsverlag, 2006.

Dell'Aversano, Carmen. "Worlds, Things, Words: Rushdie's Sytle from *Grimus* to *Midnight's Children.*" *Coterminous Worlds: Magical Realism and Contemporary Post-Colonial Literature in English.* Ed. Linguanti, Elsa, Francesco Casotti, and Carmen Concilio. Amsterdam: Rodopi, 1999. 61-69.

D'Hean, Theo L. "Magic Realism and Postmodernism: Decentering Privileged Centers." *Magical Realism: Theory, History, Community.* Ed. Lois Parkinson Zamora and Wendy B. Faris. Durham: Duke UP, 1995. 191-208.

Dissanayake, Wimal. "The Body in Indian Theory and Practice: Introduction to Part Two." *Self as Body in Asian Theory and Practice.* Ed. Thomas P. Kasulis, Roger T. Aimes and Wimal Dissanayake. Albany, NY: SUNY Press, 1993. 39–44.

Dunn, Robert G. *Identity Crises: A Social Critique of Postmodernity.* Minneapolis: U of Minnesota P, 1998.

Fokkema, Aleid. "Post-Modern Fragmentation or Authentic Essence?: Character in *The Satanic Verses.*"... *Shades of Empire in Colonial and Post-Colonial Literatures.* Ed. C.C. Barfoot and Theo D'Haen. Amsterdam: Rodopi, 1993. 51–64.

Fanon, Frantz. *Black Skin, White Masks.* New York: Grove Press, 1967.

---. *The Wretched of the Earth.* 1961. New York: Grove Press, 2004.

Faris, Wendy. "Scheherazade's Children: Magical Realism and Postmodern Fiction." *Magical Realism: Theory, History, Community.* Ed. Lois Parkinson Zamora and Wendy B. Faris. Durham: Duke UP, 1995. 163–190.

Foucault, Michel. "Nietzsche, Genealogy, History." *The Foucault Reader.* Ed. Paul Rabinow. New York: Pantheon Books, 1984.76–100.

Foster Jr., John Burt. "Magical Realism, Compensatory Vision, and Felt History: Classical Realism Transformed in *The White Hotel.*" *Magical Realism: Theory, History, Community.* Ed. Lois Parkinson Zamora and Wendy B. Faris. Durham: Duke UP, 1995. 267–283.

Giddens, Anthony. *Modernity and Self-Identity: Self and Society in the Late Modern Age.* Stanford: Stanford UP, 1991.

Gikandi, Simon. *Maps of Englishness: Writing Identity in the Culture of Colonialism.* New York: Columbia UP, 1996.

Gonzalez, Madelena. *Fiction after the Fatwa: Salman Rushdie and the Charm of Catastrophe.* Amsterdam: Rodopi, 2005.

Goonetilleke, D.C.R.A. *Salman Rushdie.* Basingstoke: Macmillan, 1998.

Gorra, Michael. *After Empire: Scott, Naipul, Rushdie.* Chicago: U of Chicago P, 1997.

Grant, Damien. *Salman Rushdie.* Plymouth: Northcote House, 1999.

Guha, Ramachandra. *India After Gandhi: The History of the World's Largest Democracy.* London: Macmillan, 2007.

Hale, David George. *The Body Politic: A Political Metaphor in Renaissance Literature.* The Hague: Mouton, 1971.

Hall, Stuart. "Cultural Identity and Diaspora." *Identity: Community, Culture, Difference.* Ed. Jonathan Rutherford. London: Lawrence and Wishart, 1998. 222–237.

---. "Introduction: Who Needs 'Identity'?" *Questions of Cultural Identity.* Ed. Stuart Hall and Paul du Gay. London: Sage, 1996. 1–17.

Hardie, Philip. "Ovid and Early Imperial Literature." *The Cambridge Companion to Ovid.* Ed. Philip Hardie. Cambridge: Cambridge UP, 2002. 34–46.

Harris, Jonathan Gil. *Foreign Bodies and the Body Politic: Discourses of Social Pathology in Early Modern England.* Cambridge: Cambridge UP, 1998.

Harvey, David. *The Condition of Postmodernity: an Enquiry into the Origins of Cultural Change.* Oxford: Blackwell, 1989.

Heffernan, Teresa. "Apocalyptic Narratives: the Nation in Salman Rushdie's *Midnight's Children.*" *Twentieth Century Literature* 46.4 (Winter 2000): 470–491.

Hogan, Patrick Colm. "*Midnight's Children*: Kashmir and the Politics of Identity." *Twentieth Century Literature* 47.4 (Winter 2001): 510–544.

"Hybridität." *Metzler Lexikon Literatur- und Kulturtheorie: Ansätze – Personen – Grundbegriffe.* Ed. Ansgar Nünning. 2nd ed. 2001.

Huddart, David. *Homi K. Bhabha*. London: Routledge, 2006.

"Identity." *The Oxford English Dictionary*. 2nd ed. 1989.

Jameson, Frederic. "Third-World Literature in the Era of Multinational Capitalism." *Social Text* 15 (Autumn 1986): 65–88.

Kane, Jane. "The Migrant Intellectual and the Body of History: Salman Rushdie's *Midnight's Children*." *Contemporary Literature* 37.1 (Spring 1996): 94–118.

Kellner, Douglas. *Media Culture: Cultural Studies, Identity and Politics between the Modern and the Postmodern*. London: Routledge, 1995.

Kennedy, Paul. "Introduction: Globalization and the Crisis of National Identities." *Globalization and National Identities: Crisis or Opportunity?* Ed. Paul Kennedy and Catherine J. Danks. Houndmills: Palgrave, 2001.

Keown, Michelle. *Postcolonial Pacific Writing*. London: Routledge, 2005.

Koller, John M. "Human Embodiment: Indian Perspectives." *Self as Body in Asian Theory and Practice*. Ed. Thomas P. Kasulis, Roger T. Aimes and Wimal Dissanayake. Albany, NY: SUNY Press, 1993. 1993. 45–58.

Kortenaar, Neil ten. *Self, Nation, Text in Salman Rushdie's* Midnight's Children. Montreal: McGill-Queen's UP, 2004.

Kuortti, Joel. *Fictions to Live in: Narration as an Argument for Fiction in Salman Rushdie's Novels*. Frankfurt a.M: Peter Lang, 1998.

Larrain, Jorge. *Ideology and Cultural Identity: Modernity and the Third World Presence*. Cambridge: Polity Press, 1994.

Leik, Robert K., and Alexandra R. Goulding. "Threats to Academic Identity and Commitment For Faculty of Power." *Self and Identity Through the Life Course in Cross-Cultural Perspective*. Ed. Timothy J. Owens. Stamford: Jai Press, 2000. 143–158.

Linguanti, Elsa. Introduction. *Coterminous Worlds: Magical Realism and Contemporary Post-Colonial Literature in English*. By Linguanti. Ed. Linguanti, Elsa, Francesco Casotti and Carmen Concilio. Amsterdam: Rodopi, 1999. 1–7.

Lucretius. *De Rerum Natura*. Trans. W.H.D. Rouse. Cambridge: Harvard UP, 1975.

Lupton, Deborah. *Medicine as Culture: Illness, Disease and the Body in Western Societies*. London: Sage, 1995.

Lützeler, Paul Michael. "Moving In Circles: Identity Formation in the Postmodern Condition." *Adventures of Identity – European Multicultural Experiences and Perspectives*. Ed. John Docker and Gerhard Fischer. Tübingen: Stauffenburg-Verlag, 2001. 1–8.

"Magic Realism." *A Dictionary of Literary Terms and Literary Theory*. J.A. Cuddon. 3rd ed. 1991.

Maldonado, Tomás. "The Body: Artificialization and Transparency." *Mediating the Human Body: Technology, Communication, and Fashion*. Ed. Leopoldina Fortunati, James Everett Katz and Raimonda Riccini.Mahwah, NJ: Lawrence Erlbaum Associates. 2003. 15–22.

Manecke, Ute. *Salman Rushdie's Concept of Wholeness in the Context of the Literature of India*. Diss. U Heidelberg, 2006.

May, Stephen, Tariq Modood, and Judith Squires. "Ethnicity, Nationalism and Minority Rights: Charting the Disciplinary Debates." *Ethnicity, Nationalism, and Minority Rights*. Ed. Stephen May, Tariq Modood and Judith Squires. Cambridge: Cambridge UP, 2004. 1–26.

McGuigan, Jim. *Culture and the Public Sphere*. London: Routledge, 1996.

McLeod, John. *Beginning Postcolonialism*. Manchester: Manchester UP, 2000.

Merivale, Patricia. "Saleem Fathered by Oskar: *Midnight's Children*, Magic Realism, and *The Tin Drum*." Ed. Lois Parkinson Zamora and Wendy B. Faris. *Magical Realism: Theory, History, Community*. Durham: Duke UP, 1995. 329–346.

Mills, James H., and Satadru Sen. Introduction. *Confronting the Body: The Politics of Physicality in Colonial and Post-Colonial India*. By Mills and Sen. London: Anthem Press, 2004. 1–15.

Mitchell, David T., and Sharon L. Snyder. *The Body and Physical Difference: Discourses of Disability*. Ann Arbor: U of Michigan P, 2000.

Miura, Noriko. *Marginal Voice, Marginal Body: The Treatment of the Human Body in the Works of Nakagami Kenji, Leslie Marmon Silko, and Salman Rushdie*. Dissertation.com, 2000.

Modood, Tariq. "New Forms of Britishness: Post-Immigration Ethnicity and Hybridity in Britain." *Identity and Integration: Migrants in Western Europe*. Ed. Rosemarie Sackmann, Bernhard Peters and Thomas Faist. Aldershot: Ashgate Publishing, 2003. 77–90.

Montserrat, Dominic. *Changing Bodies, Changing Meanings: Studies on the Human Body in Antiquity*. London: Routledge, 1998.

Nehru, Jawaharlal. "Tryst with Destiny." *The Vintage Book of Indian Writing 1947–1997*. Ed. Salman Rushdie and Elizabeth West. London: Vintage, 1997. 1–2.

Noonan, Harold W. *Personal Identity*. London: Routledge, 2003.

Ovid. *Metamorphoses*. Trans. A.D. Melville. Oxford: Oxford UP, 1998.

Papastergiadis, Nikos. *The Turbulence of Migration: Globalization, Deterritorialization and Hybridity*. Cambridge: Polity Press, 2000.

Petersson, Margareta. *Unending Metamorphoses: Myth, Satire and Religion in Salman Rushdie's Novels*. Lund: Lund UP, 1996.

Punday, Daniel. "Narrative Performance in the Contemporary Monster Story." *The Modern Language Review* 97.4. (Oct. 2002): 803–820.

Radhakrishnan, R. "Postcoloniality and the Boundaries of Identity." *Callaloo* 16.4 (Autumn 1993): 750–771.

Rocher, Rosanne. Rev. of *Indian Traffic: Identities in Question in Colonial and Postcolonial India*, by Parama Roy. *Comparative Literature Studies* 37.2 (2000): 256–260.

Rushdie, Salman. "All Things Considered: Salman Rushdie Talks About His New Book." Interview with Robert Siegel. 1996. *Salman Rushdie Interviews: A Sourcebook of His Ideas*. Ed. Pradyumna S. Chauhan. Westport: Greenwood Press, 2001. 189–192.

---. "Between God and Devil." Interview with John Mitchinson. 1988. *Salman Rushdie Interviews: A Sourcebook of His Ideas*. Ed. Pradyumna S. Chauhan. Westport: Greenwood Press, 2001. 93–98.

---. "Bookworm with Michael Silverblatt, Guest: Salman Rushdie." Interview with Michael Silverblatt. 1996. *Salman Rushdie Interviews: A Sourcebook of His Ideas*. Ed. Pradyumna S. Chauhan. Westport: Greenwood Press, 2001. 199–208.

---. "The Empire Writes Back With a Vengeance." *The London Times* 3 July 1982.

---. *Fury*. London: Cape, 2001.

---. *The Ground Beneath Her Feet*. 1999. London: Vintage, 2000.

---. "Imaginative Maps: Excerpts from a Conversation with Salman Rushdie." Interview with Una Chaudhuri. 1992. *Salman Rushdie Interviews: A Sourcebook of His Ideas*. Ed. Pradyumna S. Chauhan. Westport: Greenwood Press, 2001. 21–31.

---. "In Good Faith." *Imaginary Homelands: Essays and Criticism 1981–91*. London: Granta Books, 1992. 393–414.

---. "Interview at San Francisco State University, the Poetry Center." Interview with Sedge Thomson. 1987. *Salman Rushdie Interviews: A Sourcebook of His Ideas*. Ed. Pradyumna S. Chauhan. Westport: Greenwood Press, 2001. 75–88.

---. "The Last Sigh of Diversity." Interview with Alvaro Vargas Llosa. 1996. *Salman Rushdie Interviews: A Sourcebook of His Ideas*. Ed. Pradyumna S. Chauhan. Westport: Greenwood Press, 2001. 209–212.

---. "The Location of Brazil." *Imaginary Homelands: Essays and Criticism 1981–91*. London: Granta Books, 1992. 118–128.

---. "*Midnight's Children* and *Shame*." *Kunapipi*. 7.1 (1985): 1–19.

---. *Midnight's Children*. 1981. London: Vintage Books, 2006.

---. *The Moor's Last Sigh*. 1995. London: Vintage Books, 2006.

---. "The Moor's Last Sigh." Interview with Charlie Rose. 1996. *Conversations with Salman Rushdie. Ed. Michael R. Reder*. Jackson: U P of Mississippi, 2000.

---. "The Riddle of Midnight: India, August 1987." *Imaginary Homelands: Essays and Criticism 1981–91*. London: Granta Books, 1992. 26–36.

---. "Salman Rushdie." Interview with Eleanor Wachtel. 1992. *Salman Rushdie Interviews: A Sourcebook of His Ideas*. Ed. Pradyumna S. Chauhan. Westport: Greenwood Press, 2001. 121–135.

---. "Salman Rushdie Talks to the London Consortium about *The Satanic Verses*." Interview with Colin MacCabe. 1996. *Salman Rushdie Interviews: A Sourcebook of His Ideas*. Ed. Pradyumna S. Chauhan. Westport: Greenwood Press, 2001. 213–229.

---. *The Satanic Verses*. 1988. London: Vintage Books, 2006.

---. *Shame*. 1983. London: Vintage Books, 1995.

Said, Edward. Afterword. *Orientalism*. By Said. London: Penguin Books, 2003. 329–354.

---. *Orientalism.* 1978. London: Penguin Books, 2003.

Sanga, Jaina C. *Salman Rushdie's Postcolonial Metaphors: Migration, Translation, Hybridity, Blasphemy and Globalization.* Westport: Greenwood Press, 2001.

Scheper-Hughes, Nancy, and Margaret Lock. "The Mindful Body: a Prolegomenon to Work in Medical Anthroplogy." *Medical Anthropology Quarterly: New Series* 1.1. (1987): 6–41.

Schick, Irvin Cemil. *The Erotic Margin: Sexuality and Spatiality in Alteritist Discourse.* London: Verso, 1999.

Schultheis Alexandra W. "Postcolonial Lack and Aesthetic Promise in *The Moor's Last Sigh.*" *Twentieth Century Literature* 47.4 (Winter 2001): 569–595.

Schülting, Sabine. "Peeling Off History in Salman Rushdie's *The Moor's Last Sigh.*" *Hybridity and Postcolonialism: Twentieth Century Indian Literature.* Ed. Monika Fludernik. Tübingen: Stauffenburg Verlag, 1998. 239–260.

Shakespeare, William. *The Tragedy of King Richard III.* London: Blackie and Son, 1896.

Shilling, Chris. *The Body and Social Theory.* London: Sage, 2003.

Smale, David, ed. *Salman Rushdie* Midnight's Children/The Satanic Verses*: A Reader's Guide to Essential Criticism.* Basingstoke, Macmillan: 2001.

Snow, David. "Collective Identities and Expressive Forms." *Center for the Study of Democracy* (2001). 01 October 2001. <http://repositories.cdlib.org/csd/01-07> N. pag.

Song, Mei. "The Potentials of Using Sense-Making Methodology to Study Cultural Identity as Hybrid." Paper Presented at a Non-Divisional Workshop Held at the Meeting of the International Communication Association, New York City. May 2005. 1–7.

Strand, Eric. "Gandhian Communalism and the Midnight's Children Conference." *ELH* 72 (2005): 975–1016.

Straub, Jürgen. "Personale und Kollektive Identität: Zur Analyse eines Theoretischen Begriffs." *Identitäten.* Ed. Aleida Assmann and Heidrun Friese. Frankfurt a. M.: Suhrkamp, 1999. 73–104.

Stein, Thomas Michael. "Multikulturalität im Zeitgenössischen Englischen Roman: Salman Rushdie, Hanif Kureishi, Diran Adebayo." *Wir und das*

Fremde: Nell-Breuning Symposium Rödermark Oktober 2002. Ed. Philipp Wolf and Stefanie Rück. Münster: Lit Verlag, 2004. 177-191.

Synnott, Anthony. *The Body Social: Symbolism, Self and Society*. London: Routledge, 1993.

Taylor, Sherry. "Skinned Alive: Towards a Postmodern Pedagogy of the Body." *Postmodernism, Postcolonialism and Pedagogy*. Ed. Peter McLaren. Albert Park: James Nicholas Publishers, 1995. 101-124.

Turner, Bryan S. *The Body and Society: Explorations in Social Theory*. London: Sage, 1996.

Uprety, Sanjeev Kumor. "Disability and Postcoloniality in Salman Rushdie's *Midnight's Children* and Third-World Novels." Ed. Lennard, J. Davis. *The Disability Studies Reader*. New York: Routledge, 1997. 366-381.

Wagner, Peter."Fest-Stellungen: Beobachtungen zur sozialwissenschaftlichen Diskussion über Identität." *Identitäten*. Ed. Aleida Assmann und Heidrun Friese. Frankfurt am Main: Suhrkamp, 1999. 44-72.

Walker, Steven F. "Magical Archetypes: Midlife Miracles in *The Satanic Verses*." *Magical Realism: Theory, History, Community*. Ed. Lois Parkinson Zamora and Wendy B. Faris. Durham: Duke UP, 1995. 347-371.

Warner, Marina. *Fantastic Metamorphoses, Other Worlds: Ways of Telling the Self*. Oxford: Oxford UP, 2002.

Warren, James. "Lucretius and Greek Philosophy." *The Cambridge Companion to Lucretius*. Philip Hardie and Stuart Gillespie. Cambridge: Cambridge UP, 2007. 19-32.

"Wholeness." *The Oxford English Dictionary*. 2nd ed. 1989.

Zachariah, Benjamin. *Nehru*. London: Routledge, 2004.

Zeitfracht Medien GmbH
Ferdinand-Jühlke-Straße 7
99095 Erfurt, Deutschland
produktsicherheit@kolibri360.de